THE GOOD DOG BOOK

THE GOOD DOG BOOK

THE RESPONSIBLE OWNER'S GUIDE TO A HAPPY AND HEALTHY PET

JOAN EMBERY & NAN WEITZMAN

AVON BOOKS ◆ NEW YORK

THE GOOD DOG BOOK: THE RESPONSIBLE OWNER'S GUIDE TO A HAPPY AND HEALTHY PET is an original publication of Avon Books. This work has never before appeared in book form.

AVON BOOKS
A division of
The Hearst Corporation
1350 Avenue of the Americas
New York, New York 10019

Special Thanks

~

We would not have been able to complete *The Good Dog Book* without the support and assistance of some of the nation's leading veterinarians, nutritionists, and behaviorists. Their technical assistance and knowledge of the most current information on veterinary health, medicine, science and social issues were invaluable. We are deeply grateful to this special group of advisors, who include:

Peter Borchelt, PhD; Animal Behavior Consultants, Brooklyn, New York

Colin F. Burrows, BVetMed, PhD, MRCVS; Diplomate, American College of Veterinary Internal Medicine; Professor of Medicine, College of Veterinary Medicine, University of Florida, Gainesville, Florida

Michael S. Garvey, DVM; Diplomate, American College of Veterinary Internal Medicine, American College of Veterinary Emergency and Critical Care; Vice Chief of Staff, The Animal Medical Center, New York, New York

K.C. Hayes, DVM, PhD; Diplomate, American College of Veterinary Nutrition; Professor of Biology (Nutrition) and Director, Foster Biomedical Research Laboratory, Brandeis University, Waltham, Massachusetts

Susan K. McDonough, VMD; Founder and Owner, The Cat Hospital of Philadelphia, Philadelphia, Pennsylvania

Marc A. Rosenberg, VMD; Director, Voorhees Veterinary Clinic, Voorhees, New Jersey

Ben E. Sheffy, PhD; Caspary Professor of Nutrition, Emeritus, James A. Baker Institute for Animal Health, Cornell University, Ithaca, New York

Mark D. Finke, PhD; Director of Nutrition, ALPO Pet Center, Allentown, Pennsylvania

Mark T. Lutschaunig, VMD; Manager/Veterinarian, ALPO Pet Center, Allentown, Pennsylvania

John F. Prange, DVM; Vice President, Quality Assurance and Professional Relations, ALPO Petfoods, Inc., Allentown, Pennsylvania

Note

~

The Good Dog Book is designed to be your complete guide to responsible dog ownership. From selecting the right dog for you, to training and health care, this book will cover nearly every topic you'll ever encounter with your dog.

The book is divided logically into sections, with each section giving you a concise overview of the subject.

Contents

~

Introduction

~

Have you ever thought about the special bond that pet owners and their dogs share? Although there are many practical reasons for owning a dog, from security to companionship, most owners would agree that dogs are without peer when it comes to providing their masters and "families" with unconditional love.

Owning a dog can be one of life's greatest joys. Evolution has created in the dog a creature with an infinite capacity for devotion. In exchange for all of this, an owner need provide only equal doses of affection and discipline, along with proper nutrition and regular medical care.

As professionals who have devoted our lives to animals and human beings who care passionately about them, we are concerned about the many challenges facing dog lovers today. As we write this, the unwanted pet population in the United States is at an all time high, thousands of strays roam the streets and countless unnecessary dog attacks occur each year. Humane shelters across the country are flooded with an estimated 12 to 20 million unwanted animals, often turned in by owners who could not handle their animal's behavioral problems or unwanted litters. We're convinced many of these issues could be resolved through responsible pet ownership.

We have written *The Good Dog Book* with the hope of teaching people that well-behaved dogs begin with responsible owners, and that pet owners who are responsible will be rewarded with a gift of devotion that only a well-trained dog can offer. This book is designed to answer important questions related to successful responsible dog ownership—from selecting the dog that's right for you to effectively utilizing proven training techniques of professional breeders and animal handlers; from dealing with a variety of health care issues to the history of dogs and their unique relationship with humans through the ages.

In addition to learning about successfully raising a happy and healthy dog, you'll also be helping to solve a serious problem when you purchase this book. Thanks to a special grant from ALPO Petfoods, proceeds from *The Good Dog Book* will be donated to the Responsible Dog Owners Association, a nonprofit organization committed to teaching people to be more responsible dog owners and helping to find humane solutions to the compelling issues of unwanted pet overpopulation and pet homelessness.

We hope that you find *The Good Dog Book* enjoyable as well as educational. We had fun writing and organizing this material, since it deals with a subject—namely dogs—that we truly care about. And we believe that the information we have gathered for this book will give you the tools you need to fully experience the unique rewards of having a relationship with a happy, healthy and responsive dog.

JOAN EMBERY
NAN WEITZMAN
January 1993

THE GOOD DOG BOOK

1

Why Bother with a Dog?

OWNING A DOG TAKES EFFORT. IT'S NOT LIKE TURNING ON THE television and being entertained. You have to feed, water, walk, train and entertain your dog. Why bother?

The relationship between a person and a dog is special. A dog's love is unconditional. Your dog won't care who you are, how you look, where you live. There are dogs living with homeless people in New York who are as attached to their owners—living out of a shopping cart on the street—as the dogs owned by the wealthy inhabitants of Park Avenue co-ops. The dog doesn't care about anything but you, the most important thing in his life. As the master, you are trusted.

Your dog is your special friend and confidante. When the world seems out of control, when your life is less than perfect, your dog is there for you. He seems to understand your feelings.

Dogs can instantly change our mood, lifting us out of depressions. They can share a quiet moment, sensing the importance of it.

For people in nursing homes, hospitals and other institutions, dogs provide a source of affection and contact that can literally be life-saving. There is a wealth of anecdotal evidence to support the-

1

ories that "therapy dogs" and other animals can help people who have lost interest in life and withdrawn from human interaction regain their will to live. Recent studies show that elderly people with pets live longer—possibly because their pets' dependence on them makes them feel needed in a way that no one else can.

Dogs have helped bring autistic children out of their self-encapsulated world and have brought drug-addicted children back into society. The dog has the power to communicate without words, to share emotions.

For those who are lonely, the dog is an able companion. Dogs can give new meaning to the lives of the newly widowed who are often left without a companion.

There are many other ways in which dogs help mankind, such as assisting wheelchair-bound, blind, and hearing-impaired individuals; and working with law enforcement, search and rescue, narcotics, bomb detection; and herding of livestock.

Emotions aren't the only aspect of human life affected by dogs. They bring physical change to our lives, too. For those of us who never seem to get enough exercise, the addition of a dog to our home can be the stimulus we need to take a walk or a run once a day, every day.

Recent research shows that petting an animal lowers people's heart rate and blood pressure and calms them. Stroking your dog feels good to both you and your dog, as it relaxes the two of you.

The family pet also provides parents with an invaluable tool for teaching children about love, commitment and responsibility.

Dogs seem to know about people. They spend hours studying us and what makes us tick. They know how to motivate us to do what they want. They know what makes us happy, and what makes us mad. When they do something wrong, they seem to know—almost anticipating our response.

Dogs share their emotions with us, too. They may be protective of us when other dogs or people are around. They show affection with a lick or a long look into our eyes. They get anxious when it's time for a walk or dinner. They thrive on being presented with the challenge of a new trick or exercise to learn. They are excited when an old friend or playmate comes visiting. And they are sad when their master leaves—even for a day's work. But they'll be happy upon the return home!

The relationship you develop with your dog is a marvelous one that bonds the two of you into lasting friendship, where you are friends and companions and so much more.

Is owning a dog worth all of the time, trouble and expense? Absolutely!

~

People can learn a lot about themselves and the quality of their relationships from their pets. A dog's behavior reflects the time, love, effort, and amount of yourself you put into raising the animal. It's been my experience that the more you give, the more you get back in return.

JOAN EMBERY

2

The Case for
Responsible Dog Ownership

Twelve to twenty million unwanted animals were left at animal shelters in 1992. According to the humane organizations, 8 to 11 million of these animals were euthanized—killed—after only a few days because no one adopted them and space is limited in most shelters. If you ask your local humane society or animal shelter, you will probably find that many animals will be euthanized there this year.

The two primary reasons dogs get turned into shelters are that their owners didn't want to keep them because of behavior problems, or that the dog never had a home in the first place. Because dogs depend on their owners to provide for them, they try to let their owners know what they need—from food to a walk and from some attention to a little reassurance. When their owners don't understand what they are trying to get across, dogs may become frustrated. That frustration can lead to such unacceptable behaviors as nipping and chewing.

By the same token, people want their dogs to understand what is expected of them, despite the obvious language barrier and the differences in intellect. People often get frustrated when their dogs just don't seem to be able to learn a specific lesson, even if the command they are using for the task is different every time. As you can see, it all comes back to being able to communicate effectively to our dogs what we expect of them.

When a person gets a dog, he or she is, or should be, committing to provide for the animal's basic lifetime needs. Too many people who fall for an irresistible puppy are unprepared for the time, energy, knowledge and funds it takes to successfully raise a happy, healthy and well-disciplined dog. A well cared for dog will do its very best to please you. Being a responsible dog owner also includes preventing unplanned births and assuring that puppies from a planned litter have good homes.

Save a Dog—Adopt!

It's not necessary to spend big bucks to get a great dog. Some of the best dogs in the world are free—or nearly free! You'll conveniently find them at your local shelter. If you are willing to take on a bit of a challenge and put in a little extra effort, you can have the rewarding experience of turning a dog's life around—by saving it from being unnecessarily euthanized.

You'll find dogs of almost every shape, color and type: purebreds and mixed breeds; active and not so active dogs; fuzzy, silky, long-haired and short-haired dogs; hounds, retrievers and lap dogs; elderly dogs and puppies. The key to success with a shelter dog is to walk through the door knowing both the possibilities and the pitfalls.

Most of the dogs at a shelter are somewhat unknown quantities. The shelter staff may not know much about the dog, aside from a guess at his age and breed(s). If the dog was surrendered by a previous owner, the shelter might be able to give you a partial version of the dog's history.

A shelter dog may have health problems that his owner couldn't afford to take care of and been dropped off at the shelter in the hopes that someone with a little more money would adopt it. Or the owner could have had health problems, or died, leaving no one to care for a well-trained, perfectly healthy and loving companion.

Choosing a shelter dog is a challenge, but it's worth every bit of effort when the result is a wonderful companion for you and your family.

Adopting an animal from a shelter is not difficult. The rules may differ slightly from shelter to shelter, but the basic procedure is the same. You'll be asked several questions to help the shelter determine whether you will be a responsible pet owner, and whether you and the dog are compatible. You may be asked to make a small donation or pay a small fee that might include basic shots. Some shelters also require spaying or neutering and may give you a discount certificate to have it done by a local veterinarian or offer low-cost spaying and neutering clinics. Or they may refund all or part of the adoption fee with proof of spaying or neutering.

While puppies are very appealing, an older dog is also worth considering. With an adult dog, what you see is what you get—so you can tell how big he is and what his coat looks like and what his disposition is. A mature dog may also have had some training—such as house training—and may very well have been someone else's well cared for pet. The adult dog is more likely to be past the mischievous, hyperactive and teething stages of puppyhood. It's certainly worth asking yourself whether a mature animal might fit into your life-style better than a puppy.

When you get your dog home, remember that he has been through a series of somewhat traumatic experiences. Communication. Understanding. Patience. Discipline. Training. Love. These six elements can work to make almost any dog a good dog, no matter how he came into your life.

Solve a Problem—Spay and Neuter!

The healthy, sane and humane solution to the current unwanted pet overpopulation crisis in the United States is spaying and neutering. As the saying goes, an ounce of prevention is worth a pound of cure. Given the frightening number of homeless pets in this country and the high incidence of dog euthanasia, we should ask ourselves "why not?"—instead of "why?"—when the question of spaying or neutering arises. It is a myth that having a litter is good or necessary for a female dog, and there are no sound veterinary reasons for a male dog to procreate either.

When you spay and neuter, you become a part of the solution to the unwanted pet overpopulation crisis. Pet owners who spay and neuter their dogs are likely to be rewarded with a pet that has a better disposition and fewer health problems and is less likely to wander. Responsible pet owners understand the facts and leave dog breeding to the experts.

3

Choosing the Right Dog for You

Before You Buy a Dog

FOR MANY PEOPLE, ACQUIRING A DOG SEEMS TO BE THE RIGHT THING to do. For many of us, life just isn't complete unless a dog is along for the ride.

Letting a dog join you on life's journey is a big decision. You will be living together in the same space, eating at the same time, sharing friends and playing together. Sharing your life with a dog requires a commitment to caring for another being—one who cannot care for himself.

Think hard about whether the time really is right for you to own a dog. If you have any doubt, don't get a dog. It's not fair to the dog. Ask yourself—honestly—these questions before you purchase your first dog:

- "Is my life-style suited to the dog I want?" Each dog is different. Some get anxious if you're gone too long, destroying house and home if not confined to a safe place. Others can stay home alone for hours without a problem. Do you travel? Do you live in an apartment or a house? What else about your life-style would steer you toward or away from a particular dog's temperament.

- "Do I want this dog because of his appearance?" Too many times people base their choice of a dog on what the puppy looks like. Puppies, however, outgrow their cuteness in a matter of months. Make sure you like the way the dog will look as an adult by looking at the parents. Don't be fooled by looks. Instead, check the dog's personality. It's the dog's temperament that will elicit your affection or scorn.

- "Am I prepared for the grooming this dog will require?" Long-haired dogs require regular grooming by you or a professional. This involves time and money and some effort on your part. Are you ready for that? Are you ready for a dog that sheds, leaving hair all over your clothes, your carpet, your furniture—and even your bed?

Grooming Questions to Think About

Here are some questions to ask yourself concerning grooming and your dog:

1. Do you live in a northern, southern or moderate climate?
2. How much time are you willing to spend grooming your dog each week?
3. Who will be responsible for the dog's daily grooming?
4. Are you prepared to pay to have your dog's coat maintained by a professional groomer on a regular basis?
5. How much are you willing to spend to take your dog to a professional groomer, if needed?

A Dog for the Children

Does your child want a dog? Then you want a dog that's going to be good with children. Unfortunately, we can point to no single breed and say, "This breed is the perfect pet for a child." Dogs are the product of their environment and upbringing, so the character of the individual dog remains the most important consideration. But do compare breeds—there are differences.

Facts about your child can make a difference in the selection process. How old is your child? Is he or she emotionally mature enough to care for a dog? Is he or she physically able to handle a dog, especially a big dog?

Dog breeders are an important source of information about their dogs. Talk with them about how their dogs fit in with families and children. Other information sources abound. Read books and magazines about the breeds, and see the dogs at dog shows or obedience trials.

Regardless of the size of the dog you choose, young children should never be left unsupervised when playing with a puppy. Puppies are more interested in eating and sleeping than in roughhousing with the kids. The children may unintentionally hurt or tease the puppy, who may nip or bite the children.

No stable, well-trained adult dog should attack a child unprovoked, although not every dog will tolerate a pesky toddler who constantly prods, pokes and pulls the dog's ears or hair. Many dogs will endure the abuse or find a hiding place. Others may growl or nip. Be conscious of the dog's feelings, and keep the toddler away from the dog if necessary.

Other Factors to Think About

When thinking about the best dog for you, consider the size of the dog and his exercise needs. All dogs need exercise. Small ones can usually find enough space in a home or apartment to race around and get their exercise. Of course, larger dogs need exercise, too. Long walks and outdoor time spent playing or chasing will keep any dog happy. Exercise needs are based on the size and breed of the dog. Small breeds may need only a brisk walk around the neighborhood, while sporting breeds may require a walk of several miles a day.

Let's say that you don't give your dog enough exercise. What can happen? The truth is many of the behavior problems people think are not solvable are a result of inadequate exercise. Dogs who are well exercised will sleep between exercise periods. Those suffering from inadequate exercise will find ways to release their excess energy—such as chewing up the furniture or walls. The energy has to go somewhere, so you are obviously better off getting into the habit of enjoying nice long walks with your dog.

If you work, exercising your dog is only one of the problems you will need to overcome. The typical workday, with commuting time added, makes for a long stretch for your dog to sit home alone. One solution is to come home on your lunch hour to let your dog out. Another is a well-fenced yard, with a doggy door.

The nine-to-five dog may suffer. Accidents can happen, despite being housebroken, if he is unable to relieve himself. Loneliness and inactivity can lead to boredom and destructiveness. He may even get depressed. A companion to play with can help, as two dogs can always find something to keep themselves occupied.

Some dogs are self-exercisers. They'll find any excuse to have fun and run madly around the house or yard. You don't have to worry about these hyperkinetic dogs getting their fill of exercise.

The bottom line: Get a dog who reflects your own exercise needs. If you love to get out and enjoy the changing scenes of nature, get a dog who will look forward to the daily explorations. If you can't get out and walk daily, get an older dog who sleeps much of the day.

All dogs need directed exercise such as a walk through the park or chasing a ball that you throw. When deciding on a dog, consider the environment you will be providing. Is your yard big or small (or nonexistent)? How big is your house? Is it located in an urban, suburban or rural location? What type of house or apartment do you live in?

Let's look at living quarters for your dog. Will the dog be kept inside the house or outside only? Dogs like human companionship, and that's usually not part of the picture out in the backyard. So plan on spending a lot of time with your dog.

When the dog is outside, he should be confined and supervised. A fence is the best bet for keeping your dog in your yard. Chains get tangled, and an excited dog can break them. Fences are much more efficient at keeping your dog in and visiting dogs out.

If your dog is going to be outside for long periods, you must make sure that shade and water are available.

What about responsibility for the dog? Who will be responsible for exercising the dog, and how much time will be spent exercising him? Who will be in charge of the puppy—supervising the puppy's playtime and discipline, feeding, training, grooming and health care?

Being responsible for your dog means finding someone to care for him when you have to go out of town. Does your job require much traveling? Do you take long or frequent vacations? You need to locate a boarding kennel or a neighbor to care for your dog while you are away.

The activity level of your household is another important factor. You'll want to match the energy level of the dog with the activity level of the household. Are you very active, somewhat active or not active at all? How many young children do you have?

Think, too, about the size of your perfect dog. Toy breeds are thirteen inches or less, small breeds are fourteen to eighteen inches, medium breeds are nineteen to twenty-six inches and the larger breeds are twenty-seven inches and over. (All measurements are shoulder height.)

One-Person Dogs

Some breeds are known as one-person dogs. They usually form strong bonds with one member of the household more than with other family members. The dog will usually pay attention and respond with more affection to this person.

Other, more independent breeds may not form any strong bonds with the family and are aloof. They may not be well-suited for life with a large family.

Still other breeds thrive on the affection of a large family. They probably will form equally strong bonds with all the members of the family. These breeds will most likely greet a stranger with the same amount of affection and respect as a family member.

How the dog reacts in family life depends on the individual dog and how the dog is raised.

Dominant and Submissive Dogs

Within every breed, even within a single litter, is a whole range of dominant and submissive behavior. Dogs will establish a hierarchy among themselves, beginning as early as four weeks of age. We must help them find their place in the hierarchy of the human family, too. This means that you must determine whether you are dominant or submissive, as your personality affects your relationship with your dog. If you are attracted to one of the more dominant types of dog, it is imperative that you and the rest of your family are able to remain the boss should your authority be challenged by the dog.

If a submissive dog is more to your liking, you must be careful not to be too harsh with the dog. Being overly dominant with a submissive dog can lead to a number of behavior problems. The most common is the "fear biter." This dog feels totally threatened by a situation, and his only means of protecting himself is to bite.

Guard Versus Watch Dogs

You may want a watch dog, an alarm, to warn the family of probable threats. Do you know the difference between a watch dog and a guard dog? A guard dog is not a trained attack dog. He is very possessive of his environment and his family and will not greet a stranger as a family member. A watch dog is there to sound the alarm, while a guard dog may or may not bark before he acts on the perceived threat. Most dogs make good watch dogs, but not all dogs make good guard dogs.

Let's look at a few typical breed characteristics. The Collie is good for a small family. It has a submissive temperament. It makes a good watch dog, but a poor guard dog. The Dalmatian is also a good dog for a small family, but it is less submissive and a bit more dominant. It is both a good watch dog and a good guard dog. The Rottweiler has even more of a dominant personality. This makes it both a good watch dog and guard dog. It is more comfortable with just one master, as opposed to a family situation. The Chow Chow is also a one-person dog. It has a dominant temperament and is both a good watch dog and an excellent guard dog. Then there are dogs like the Bulldog. They're happy with a large family. With an intermediate temperament, the Bulldog is a good watch dog, but a poor guard dog.

Shelters

Where do you find the right dog for you? There are three places to consider: shelters, pet shops and breeders.

The local animal shelter or pound has many animals waiting for homes. You may not get a purebred, but you might find a companion for life. You'll definitely save a life in the process.

Shelter pets do need special consideration. For example, there is no guarantee on a puppy's adult size or looks. Your veterinarian or the shelter people may be able to help estimate the puppy's adult size and appearance.

It is important to make sure the adoptee is healthy. Don't adopt an animal who is ill. You'll spend a great deal of money, time and heartache on an animal who may never be well.

Personality needs to be taken into account, whether you adopt a puppy or an adult dog. Shelter animals may not have had proper socialization, training or housebreaking. They may also be frightened by their current surroundings. However, in a different setting, with care and understanding, they could become great dogs.

Many dogs have been given to the shelter because they developed a problem in the relationship in their prior home. This problem may have been caused by insufficient training or irresponsible pet ownership. You should keep this in mind when you choose to adopt this dog as it may require additional attention to become a good pet.

Shelters often require the animal be neutered or spayed before he can be adopted. This is a good idea for any dog. To make it easy, some shelters offer low-cost spay/neuter clinics. Others will refund part of the adoption fee once you have had the procedure done by a veterinarian. Spaying or neutering helps eliminate accidental pregnancies and unwanted puppies and keeps the animal shelter population under control.

There are many good books on the subject of adopting a pet from the shelter. Two are written by Carol Lea Benjamin, *The Chosen Puppy* and *The Second-Hand Dog*.

Pet Shop Puppies

Pet stores are a convenient source of puppies. They're not always the best source, though. Pet store puppies usually have gone from breeder to broker to distributor to store. The dogs probably have traveled great distances, and through many hands, and were separated from their siblings at too early an age, creating stress, which can lead to behavioral and health problems. Family history may be unknown as well as the quality of the parents. You may not know what the parents looked like or what personality they had. You cannot see how well or poorly fed they were, what medical attention they received or at what age the puppies were removed from their mother.

Inquire about the source of the pet store puppies and follow up if possible to confirm. There are people who consider themselves to be private breeders but in reality are mass producing puppies for sale at pet stores. Even when breeders sell to pet stores, you may not be able to meet the parents.

Remember, you are looking for a companion to share your life with. The best way to see what you are getting yourself into is to see the parents.

How to Find a Purebred Puppy

We chose a lab because it matched our life-style: We are athletic, outdoor people. Traveler was the perfect choice for us because she requires minimal grooming and has a great temperament with all the different people, film crews, and animals on our ranch.

JOAN EMBERY

If you have made the decision to get a purebred dog, one of the best places to begin your search is a large dog show. You'll be able to see hundreds of dogs of many breeds. You'll see their size and demeanor as adults and the amount of grooming they require.

Most areas have at least two dog shows a year, and many of them are free to the public. To find out where and when your local dog shows occur, ask a knowledgeable local dog breeder or trainer, or write the Show Plans Dept., American Kennel Club, 51 Madison Ave., New York, NY 10010; 212-676-8200. In Canada, contact the Canadian Kennel Club, 100-89 Skyway Ave., Etobkoke, Ontario M9W6RY; 416-675-5511.

At the show, look for breeds that interest you. It's fine to wander around "behind the scenes." If owners or handlers are not busy getting ready to go into the show ring, talk to them about their dogs. Don't be offended if they don't have time to talk, though. Showing a dog is serious business to them and getting their dog just right is important. You can visit with them after they've exhibited the dog or take their business card and call another day. After deciding on the breed or breeds you like, make appointments to visit the kennels.

Choosing the Breeder

Choosing a breeder is as important as choosing the purebred dog. The breeder is your guide in selecting the right dog and in solving all the little problems that crop up as you raise a puppy. The breeder is your most valuable source of information about a breed, before and after you get the dog. She can tell you if the dogs are strong willed, what health problems are typical in the breed and what specific care might be required. The breeder will be your main guide through the first-time jitters and crises. Make sure this is someone to whom you can relate.

As you talk to the breeder, you'll want to decide if this is the right guide for you. The breeder's kennel should be clean and pleasant, with no offensive odors, and the breeder should be nice, polite and helpful.

Ask why the breeder chose the breed. You should be able to sense the knowledge, caring and concern for the breed. Find out what she likes about the breed, and what she doesn't like.

Ask the breeder why she breeds dogs. Is she interested in bettering the breed, or is she just in it to make a little extra pocket money? Does she belong to the national breed club and the local kennel club? Does she subscribe to the code of ethics of the national club? And does she exhibit her dogs at dog shows? These questions will help you determine if she is truly a responsible breeder, someone who cares intensely about her dogs and who seeks to improve the breed.

Next, ask about the available dogs. Find out why she bred the litter and what physical problems the dogs might have.

Check the level of health care her dogs receive. They should be vaccinated and dewormed regularly and in good overall condition. This line of questioning should lead you to believe that this breeder cares for the health and well-being of her dogs.

Ask about the paperwork that comes with the puppies. Does she have the American Kennel Club registration forms (puppy blue slips)? If not, your dog may not be eligible for registration with the AKC.

Warning Signs

Avoid breeders who let puppies go before six weeks of age. Some states require the puppy to stay even longer with the mother. This time period a pup spends with its littermates and mom helps it become adjusted as an adult.

Ask the breeder if she refunds money or will replace the puppy if it turns out to have a physical problem. Will she take the puppy back if he just doesn't work out? A good, reputable breeder will insist that the puppy be returned if you can't keep him.

Avoid "backyard breeders" as your source of purebred puppies. The puppies may have been the result of an accidental pregnancy or produced to show the kids "the miracle of birth." Maybe the dog was being given "the experience of a litter" before being spayed. These are all inappropriate reasons to have puppies, and this person will not be able to supply you with expert information and guidance.

If you have any doubts about the quality of the breeder's dogs, ask for the names of owners of her other puppies—and call them! If this is a first litter, call and talk to the breeder's veterinarian about the health and quality of the puppies and of the breeder's care for her other pets.

A good, reputable breeder will be checking you out, too. The breeder will ask you plenty of questions to make sure that your home is right for her precious puppy. This rigorous questioning will indicate that she cares where her puppies go and how you will do as a parent.

Make the effort to find the best dog and the best breeder. It will pay off in the long run with a dog who makes you happy!

——————————— Checklist ———————————

Common Questions Asked by Breeders and Shelters

Owning a dog is a big responsibility and requires you to make calculated decisions. The following questions have been provided to help you in your decision-making process. They are typically asked by breeders or shelters to help you focus on the type of dog that is right for you.

1. Type of area you live in: a) urban b) suburban c) rural
2. Size of yard: a) less than ¼ acre b) ¼ to 1 acre c) more than 1 acre
3. Home (rent or own): a) apartment b) two-family home c) single-family home
4. Size of home interior: a) 500 sq. ft. b) 1,000 sq. ft. c) 2,000 sq. ft.
5. Number of adults eighteen years or older living in your household: a) 1 b) 2 c) 3 +
6. Number of children under the age of ten in your household: a) 0 b) 1 c) 2 +
7. Number of children between the ages of eleven and seventeen: a) 0 b) 1 c) 2 +
8. Number of working adults in your household: a) 0 or retired b) 1 c) 2 +
9. Number of adults home during the hours of 9 A.M. and 5 P.M.: a) 0 b) 1 c) 2 +

10. Number of hours during the day the dog will be left alone:
    a) 8 + b) 5–7 c) less than 4

11. How would you describe your home's social activity level
    (e.g., parties, visiting friends, children's overnight guests,
    etc.)? a) high b) medium c) low

12. Are you planning to move? a) no b) in 1–6 months
    b) in 7–12 months c) in more than a year

13. What type of climate do you live in? a) cool (northern)
    b) moderate c) hot (southern)

14. Do you have a fenced-in yard? a) yes b) no

15. Is there shade available for the dog when he is outside?
    a) yes b) no If no, will you provide a shaded area? a) yes
    b) no

16. How many hours a day are you willing to exercise your dog?
    a) less than 1 b) 2 + hours

17. Who will be in charge of feeding the dog? a) child
    b) teenager c) adult

18. Who will be in charge of exercising/walking the dog? a) child
    b) teenager c) adult

19. Who will be in charge of the puppy's training (e.g., house-
    breaking, leash-training, etc.)? a) child b) teenager c) adult

20. Who will be in charge of the puppy's playtime, socializing,
    discipline? a) child b) teenager c) adult

21. How would you describe the stress level of your job? a) high
    b) moderate c) low

22. Does your job require traveling? a) 21% + b) 11 to 20%
    c) 0 to 10%

23. How many vacations do you take each year? a) 1 b) 2 c) 3 +

24. Do you intend to take the dog with you on vacation? a) no
    b) yes c) day trips

25. Have you located a boarding kennel or a neighbor who will
    care for the dog while you're away? a) no b) yes

26. Do you know how much it will cost to board the type of dog
    you are interested in (e.g., boarding a large dog, one hundred
    pounds or over, may cost $10.00/day)? a) no b) yes

27. Have you ever owned a dog before? a) no b) yes c) yes, our family had a dog
28. What breed or type of dog did you own or grow up with?
29. What happened to your last dog?
30. Do you presently own a dog? a) no b) yes
31. If yes to question 30, please answer the following questions.
    a. How old is it?
    b. Male or female?
    c. Neutered or spayed?
    d. Breed?
    e. Has it been around other dogs and animals? a) no b) yes
    f. Where did you purchase your dog? a) small hobby breeder b) pet store c) large kennel d) other
    g. Is the dog obedience-trained? a) no b) yes
    h. Have any of your neighbors complained about your dog? a) no b) yes
    i. Have you ever complained about a neighbor's dog being a nuisance? a) no b) yes
32. Have you ever obedience-trained a dog before? a) no b) yes
33. Do you think it is permissible to allow your dog to run loose? a) no b) yes
34. Do you know the zoning laws for the area in which you live? a) no b) yes
35. Do you know your area's dog control laws (e.g., vaccinations, license, etc.)? a) no b) yes
36. Have you located a veterinarian for the dog? a) no b) yes
37. Will the dog live in the house as a family member? a) no b) yes
38. Will the dog be an outside dog only? a) no b) yes
39. Does everyone in the house want the dog? a) no b) yes

40. Are you prepared to meet the financial responsibility of owning a dog? a) no b) yes

41. What size dog do you want to own? a) large 27 +" b) medium 19" to 26" c) small 14" to 18" d) toy 13" or less

42. What length of hair do you want your dog to have? a) long b) medium c) short

43. Are you prepared to take your medium- or long-haired dog to a groomer to have its coat properly maintained? a) no b) yes

44. Who will be in charge of the daily grooming of the dog? a) child b) teenager c) adult

45. What type of dog do you want to own? a) show dog b) companion, household pet c) hunting dog

46. What type of temperament would you like your dog to have when he greets a strange visitor for the first time? a) aloof b) friendly, outgoing c) independent

47. What type of activity level would you like in a dog? a) high (constantly wants to play) b) medium c) low (couch potato)

48. Do you want a male or a female? a) male b) female

49. Will you neuter or spay this dog? a) no b) yes

50. How familiar are you with the breed of dog you want to acquire (size at maturity, weight, plus grooming, exercise and feeding requirements)? a) not at all b) somewhat (a friend has one) c) very familiar (owned one before)

51. Are you aware of any reason why you should not own this particular breed? (e.g., health, temperament, etc.)? a) no b) yes

52. Have you read any literature on this breed of dog or any other type of informative material about caring for dogs? a) no b) yes

53. Why do you want a dog? a) peace of mind b) criminal deterrent, protection c) to teach the children the responsibility of owning a dog d) lifelong companion/friend

There are no right or wrong answers to these questions but you should be prepared to answer any and all of them when you go to speak to breeders or visit animal shelters. More important, these are questions you should ask yourself when choosing a type or size of dog, or even when determining if dog ownership is for you.

See the Parents Before You Choose

All puppies are cute. How can you tell how they will turn out? To see the future of your puppy, look closely at the whole family.

Puppies are like their parents. It pays to look at the dam (mother) and sire (father). If you can't see the parents, you're buying an unknown quantity. That's one of the big problems with buying a puppy at a pet store or adopting one from a shelter.

Mom might be real sweet, but dad could be a terror, so find out about him, too. If the parents are show dogs, dad may live in another state. If you can't meet him, ask the breeder to show you any other relatives of the puppy that she owns. Otherwise, you'll have to take the breeder's word on dad's personality.

Now, look at mom. She should be friendly and happy with her tail wagging. Her coat may be a little thin, but then, she just had pups. For the same reason, she might need to gain a bit of weight. But overall, she should look healthy and energetic. Don't worry if the dam is wary of you at first. She should calm down as soon as it is apparent you aren't going to hurt her puppies.

Meeting the puppy's grandparents, great-grandparents and elderly relatives can add more pieces to the puzzle of what your puppy will grow up to be like. Check the relatives to see if they are happy and healthy. Do they bounce up to you, tails wagging and eyes trusting? Don't buy puppies who have apprehensive, sulky or snappy relatives. Chances are the puppies will grow up to be apprehensive, sulky or snappy, too.

If all the breeder's dogs are happy, healthy, and outgoing chances are the puppy you are thinking of buying should be, too. However, this is only a starting point for making your decision. It is important to remember that a dog's behavior reflects how it is raised.

4

Your Puppy and You

WHEN YOU PURCHASE A DOG, BE SURE TO GET THE REGIS-
tration application and a signed bill of sale. These are both important
documents.

The bill of sale should include the dog's color and sex, date of
birth and names of the dog's parents. If the parents are purebreds,
their registration numbers should be included on the bill of sale.
Other information that should be on this form is a list of any vaccinations and deworming medication given and the dates.

If they think the dog is of "show quality," some breeders may
ask you to "co-own" the dog so *they* can show the dog at dog
shows. Unless you are already involved in showing dogs, don't
make complicated ownership arrangements. Buy the dog as a pet
and keep him as a pet.

Registering Your Dog

Registering your dog with the American Kennel Club, the United
Kennel Club or the Canadian Kennel Club (or another registry)

23

enables your dog to be shown at dog shows and maintains his status as a "purebred" for breeding purposes. It also confirms that you are the owner of the dog. Read the instructions carefully when you fill out the registration application. Don't forget to sign the application and enclose the correct fee. The formal registered name and registration number must be used on all correspondence with the AKC, so make a copy of the application before you mail it in.

If you have questions concerning the registration process call the AKC's Registration Office: (919) 233-9767, Monday through Friday, 8:30 A.M. to 6:30 P.M. eastern standard time.

To register a dog with either the United Kennel Club, the American Kennel Club, or the Canadian Kennel Club, he must have a pedigree—a family tree—which shows that the dog's ancestors were purebred and registered in a recognized stud book. Some breeders will sell a dog without his registration papers for less money. If your dog is registrable, do it! Registering your dog means his name and registration number are his alone and on record for all time.

What Is a Pedigree?

The pedigree is the record of your dog's ancestors, the family tree, which you can acquire from most breeders. It usually contains at least four generations. The pedigree is most useful because it allows you to trace your dog's genetic history.

Show or Pet Quality?

Most purebred puppies are pet quality. This is not because they have anything wrong with them, but because of minor points that would prevent them from a successful show career. For example, they may grow up to be too small, or too tall; their color isn't just the right shade, or maybe they have a kink in their tail.

Many breeders sell pet-quality puppies on the condition that they never be used for breeding. Some may sell them without their registration papers to discourage them from being bred. These dogs are just as purebred as their show-quality littermates and perfectly desirable as loving companions.

At What Age Should You Buy a Puppy?

The first weeks of a puppy's life are critical. Time spent exploring the environment and socializing with littermates and people shape the dog's personality and temperament. Thus, a pup should not be removed from the litter before six weeks of age.

Here's a quick timetable of puppy development. A puppy can't see until he is two weeks old and can't hear until he is three weeks of age. The puppy's motor skills develop next, followed by communication skills. The next step is learning about other dogs. Socializing in the litter includes climbing on each other, pouncing, pawing, licking, chewing, biting, growling and fighting. This "play" time is important, as information learned from relationships during this early period are building blocks for adult social behavior.

Socializing is important, too, as the puppy learns which behaviors are acceptable, which are pleasurable and which are painful. Through these lessons, the puppy learns to use the correct behavior for each situation.

The puppy will also interact with people at this stage just as with his littermates, assuming he has not been isolated from people. This all helps when training time arrives. Through your patience, guidance and understanding of canine behavior, your puppy will learn the correct behaviors.

Puppies from pet shops or puppy farms are less likely to have had the opportunity to extensively socialize with people or littermates. It is extremely important to expose these puppies to a variety of other dogs and people.

Puppy-Proofing Your Home

Before you bring your puppy home you should make sure his new environment is safe. Go from room to room, puppy-proofing the space. Remove anything at puppy level that might be hazardous if chewed on. Confine the puppy to a small area within the house, such as the laundry room or kitchen. Don't leave cigarette butts or peanut shells in ashtrays or small dishes where your puppy can get to them. If eaten, they can give your puppy an upset stomach. Secure all electrical cords, speaker wires or other types of cable to the baseboard or make them inaccessible. They make fun chew toys but can cause harmful electric shock burns and even death.

Never leave burning candles where your dog can get to them. This includes the kitchen counter, where your dog can jump up to see them, or the coffee table, where his tail may come in contact with the flame. The brightness of the flame and its flickering motion will attract him no matter where it is.

Keep all medication, cleaning fluids and the like out of your dog's way. Child-proof containers were not made to keep teething puppies safe from their contents.

Never keep the dog's treats or biscuits in the same place you store poisons. The puppy just may figure out how to open the cabinet to get a treat and grab the bottle of cleaning fluid instead.

Never leave the toilet seat lid open, especially if you use a toilet bowl cleaner. Toilet bowl cleaners are alkaline and are tempting for dogs to drink. Needless to say, this would be extremely hazardous to his health. Better yet, unless everyone in your house can remember to keep the toilet seat down, don't use a toilet bowl cleaner. Unfortunately, dogs love the ever-flowing water bowl, so make every effort to keep it clean and closed.

Keep all closet and cellar doors closed. Dogs are just as curious and as vulnerable as young children. Keeping closet doors closed keeps puppy from finding your best leather shoes.

Second-story windows should be kept closed, especially if your house has low windowsills.

Don't invite other pets into your house until your puppy has been fully vaccinated. A puppy's resistance to infection is lower than that of an adult dog. Also, don't let your puppy visit at someone else's house unless you know that dog has been vaccinated and dewormed.

Cover the trash can. Chicken bones, turkey bones and even steak bones can injure a dog if swallowed. A small chip can get lodged in the roof of his mouth or cause serious damage to his intestinal tract. Trash picking is an undesirable pastime for both dogs and puppies. Make sure the trash is secure, so that even if knocked over, the contents will not spill out.

Never leave your sewing or knitting items within a dog's reach. Remember, dogs explore many things with their noses. A curious puppy may even swallow the items.

Puppy-proofing should be extended to your garage, too. Make

Puppy-Proofing Checklist

What To Do With Hazards	Reason Why
Secure electrical cords, speaker wires, or any type of cable.	Fun to chew for puppies and can cause electrical shock.
Keep burning candles out of reach.	Bright flame and flickering motion can not only burn puppy, but could also tip over and catch fire.
Lock cabinets with medicines and cleaning fluids.	Puppies can open doors and get into cleaners and medicines that look like candy and are poisonous.
Remove peanuts, cigarette butts, chocolate from view.	Peanuts and cigarette butts can upset puppy's stomach. Chocolate can be fatal/toxic to dogs.
Close toilet lids.	Toilet bowl cleaners contain hazardous chemicals which dogs can drink.
Shut closets, cabinets, cellar doors.	Shoes, toys and tools are fun for puppies to chew, but expensive to replace.
Cover trash cans.	Chicken bones, turkey bones, and steak bones can splinter and choke a dog or injure his stomach lining if swallowed.
Remove sewing or knitting items from view.	Shiny needles can be painful if poked with a paw or even more serious if swallowed.
Put away antifreeze.	Tastes like candy to dogs and puppies and is fatal, even in the smallest amount, if swallowed.
Remove pesticides, insecticide strips, fly paper.	Toxins are hazardous or fatal to puppies.
Keep all holiday decorations: Indian corn, gourds, Christmas ornaments out of reach.	Very attractive to puppies and are fun to play with but are dangerous if eaten.
Keep household plants: Rhododendron, Japanese yew, Lily of the Valley, Poinsettias, peach and cherry pits out of reach.	Can upset dogs' stomachs and are possibly fatal if eaten.

absolutely certain that antifreeze is out of reach. Any drippings should be cleaned up immediately. Hosing the antifreeze off the garage floor or driveway is ineffective unless the spot has dried up. If you hose it for a few seconds, all you'll have done is made a larger, more enticing puddle. Antifreeze is a deadly poison. One lick is all it takes, even if all he's done is walked through the puddle and licked his paws. (If you suspect that your puppy has consumed some antifreeze, contact your veterinarian immediately!) It is better to throw cat litter on the antifreeze to absorb it, then sweep it up and put it in the trash can. Never allow a puppy in the garage while you are working or in a room where you are using power tools unless someone is there to watch him.

Pesticides are designed to kill insects. Unfortunately, they can also sicken or kill puppies. Read the label on all pesticides and follow the instructions carefully. Hanging strips, fly paper and other exposed toxins must be kept out of reach.

Refrain from being antibug happy, even when it comes to killing fleas. Mixing flea collars with flea shampoos and tick dips can be a deadly combination. Your dog can develop a severe reaction to all the products if used at the same time. Find a product you like, carefully follow the directions and stick to a schedule, and you shouldn't have any flea or tick problems.

Keep small objects out of reach. Especially during the holiday season. Indian corn, gourds and the like make inappropriate but tempting chewing toys. They have been waxed and treated with various other substances to make them last longer which can be hazardous to your puppy.

Even more dangerous are Christmas ornaments. Keep all of them out of reach. You can trim your tree as usual, just start at least a foot higher than the puppy's head. Again, these ornaments may be fun to play with or chew on, but the hazard of shattered glass is obvious. Christmas lights, ornaments and tinsel all need to be kept above puppy level.

Use barricades or child gates to keep the puppy confined to his safe room. This can solve plenty of problems no matter what the time of year.

Keep your puppy away from toxic plants. Rhododendron, Japanese yew, lily of the valley, and poinsettia as well as peach and cherry pits can all cause problems if eaten.

What to Teach Your Puppy First

Once you have your puppy home, the lessons can begin. Love is the first lesson. The puppy must be comfortable with you and have the same type of social relationship with you that he had with his mother and littermates. During the first few days a puppy is home, love, pet, stroke, cuddle and snuggle. The more he knows he is loved, the easier he will be to train.

Teach respect by respecting the puppy's needs. Provide the puppy with his own house—a crate—and his own temporary living quarters somewhere safe inside your house.

Naming Your Puppy

Traveler was a gift from ALPO when I became the company's spokeswoman. She got her name because she traveled about as far as she could go: from the ALPO Pet Center in Pennsylvania to our ranch in San Diego.

Traveler has lived up to her name because she goes almost everywhere with us. Since we are on the road a lot, she was crate trained as a puppy and is now relaxed and comfortable when traveling—in the trucks, motor home, car, golf cart and horse wagon. Not only does our dog travel readily, she's hurt when she's not asked to go. If it's got wheels, she's game.

JOAN EMBERY

The way people come up with names for dogs defies explanation. There are books with suggested pet names, just as there are baby-naming books. But it's just as easy to independently create something fitting and meaningful to your family.

You might find it helpful to give your dog a two-syllable name. Since most commands are one syllable, a two-syllable name helps the dog learn to differentiate the name from a command.

Teach the name by using it often and saying it in a bright, cheerful and happy tone. Use the puppy's name to get his attention or when playing, petting or hugging. Always associate the name with good things and never with bad things. For example, if you use the puppy's name and "Come!" at feeding time, he'll learn his name and to come when called. He'll expect good things, such as dinner, when he responds to his name and the come command.

Never use his name when you are about to discipline him. The dog must come when called and not run away. If he associates his name with bad things, he will not come. This is the biggest mistake new owners make! Again, don't use the dog's name when correcting the dog.

There's more to communication than using your voice. Since dogs don't use their voice much, nonverbal communication is important. While your dog is still young begin to establish nonverbal channels of communication. You can do this by encouraging your puppy to look at you. Look at your puppy, say his name, and when you have his attention, praise him. Then keep his attention focused on your eyes. Cradle his face and look into his eyes, telling him he is wonderful. He will soon learn your facial expressions: a smile for approval, a frown for disapproval. Watch his expressions, too. You'll understand what he wants by the look in his eye, the wrinkle of his brow or the way he is standing.

Choosing a Veterinarian

When a baby arrives in your family, you choose a pediatrician. When a dog arrives in your family, you choose a veterinarian. You want one who is conveniently located, with a good reputation and reasonable rates. Ask people with dogs which veterinarian they use and why. Call to schedule an appointment to discuss policies and visit the clinic/hospital. Try different veterinarians until you find one you like.

Don't waste time. Choose a veterinarian right away and have your dog vaccinated against the important dog diseases. Many puppies suffer from intestinal parasites or worms. They're not a big deal to treat or prevent, so have your dog checked for parasites.

A good veterinarian will put you and your dog at ease. Your veterinarian should explain health conditions, procedures, and medications in a way you can understand and will answer questions without making you feel stupid. It is of critical importance that your veterinarian provide services for emergencies.

Health Care Schedule for Puppies

Arrange with your veterinarian for the critical first series of vaccinations. These include vaccinations for distemper, hepatitis, leptospirosis, parainfluenza, rabies, canine parvovirus and coronavirus. These are major diseases that can sicken or kill a dog. Many of the vaccines are given in a single shot, but some require a series of injections over a few weeks for full protection. Annual boosters may be needed to maintain immunity.

Why Train Your Dog?

What's cute behavior for puppies can grow into a problem as they get older. When Traveler was a puppy, I let her leap into my lap. Later, when she became full grown I had to retrain her so she would not jump on peoples' laps. This was evident after we had a visitor sitting on the couch and out of nowhere our seventy pound lab catapulted herself onto his lap. Our guest was shocked to say the least.

JOAN EMBERY

~

A poorly behaved, ill-mannered dog can be a problem for everyone. Ill-behaved dogs are difficult to live with, and an uncontrollable dog can be a nuisance to the neighborhood. Loose, roaming dogs are in constant danger from cars and can be a traffic hazard to people and vehicles.

There is no good reason for having an untrained dog. All dogs should be completely house-trained and able to heel on the leash, sit, stay and come when called. It's very easy to teach basic manners, particularly when the dog is a puppy and hasn't developed any bad habits. We'll give you specific ways to train your dog later in the book. For now, just know that it is important to train your dog—beginning now and continuing throughout the dog's life.

Think about your own list of things you would like your dog to do or not do. Whatever it is you want your dog to do, remember that your dog must be well behaved and acceptable to friends and family. Training makes it possible.

Prevent Jumping Early

Jumping on people is a problem that occurs later in life but that can be prevented early. Jumping is natural for dogs—they like to kiss you on the face, and if you're not down at their nose level, they will do their best to meet you at yours!

The best solution to jumping dogs is early training: Don't ever let your puppy start. That cute, tiny puppy jumping up to kiss you quickly turns into a heavy dog with a bad habit of knocking people off balance, getting muddy paws all over expensive clothes.

Treat the problem before it becomes a big problem. Use verbal commands such as "Down" or "Off." A larger or older, more exuberant dog can be knocked off balance with a jerk of the knee to his chest or sternum. Give the down or off command and again follow with "good dog!" (Be careful where you place your knee—don't injure your dog!) Many trainers suggest *gently* stepping on the dog's back paws when he is standing upright against you. Or a tiny dog may be pushed down by carefully nudging him with your foot.

Another method is to grasp the two front paws as the dog jumps up. Most dogs will pull away immediately and become upset that you are holding on. Let go and say "down" or "off." When the dog is back on all fours, praise him with a happy "good dog!"

You can also get your dog off balance without physical contact. If you are quicker than the dog, you can simply move out of the path of the jump by pivoting. Again, give the command and the praise.

Anticipating the behavior is another possibility. Watch the dog's eyes. If your dog is trained to lie down or sit and stay, use those commands immediately and do not acknowledge or greet the dog until he is sitting still. When the dog is sitting still, praise and greet him by bending over to pet him. Be persistent. This method takes time. Just remember not to acknowledge or greet the dog until he is lying down or sitting.

Always maintain the proper sequence of positive reinforcement, giving a command, then praising with a cheerful "good dog!" and a pat on the head when the dog responds to the command properly.

Early Basic Puppy Training

I remember the two A.M. *wake-up calls and being outside in the freezing cold. I'd sit there and wait and wait while the puppy would be sniffing and playing with leaves and grabbing up branches off trees. She would look at me as if to ask "Wanna play?" and I'd look and say, "Hurry up," so we could go back to sleep.*

JOAN EMBERY

~

The wild canine pack has a hierarchy of leaders and followers. One male and one female are usually leaders; all the other canines in the pack are subordinate. Communication in the pack is based on body posture or body language. The domesticated dog uses similar means to communicate with his pack, the human family. Your understanding and recognition of these signs will help you successfully raise your puppy to be a good canine citizen.

House Training

At an early age puppies develop certain bathroom habits that later make house training easy. Very young puppies eat, sleep and relieve themselves and do little else. At this stage the mother makes sure the nest is free from excrement so the puppies don't eat in the same place they relieve themselves. Once the puppies are more mobile, they will begin to leave the nest or sleeping area to urinate or defecate. As they become more aware of their surroundings they will sniff and investigate before they relieve themselves.

Here are some points to remember when house training your dog. Puppies are unlikely to soil their eating or sleeping areas. If you give them a sleeping area—such as a crate—they will be less likely to defecate or urinate there.

Puppies use body language to say, "I am looking for a place to go to the bathroom" by sniffing and investigating an area. If you watch for the signs and rush them to a safe area to relieve themselves, house training will happen automatically.

It's important to remember that many puppies arrive at their new home at the age of eight weeks. Physiologically, they can't control their bowel movements or urination until they're twelve weeks of age. They simply can't hold it! So for those first four weeks you must teach your dog by association. While your puppy may not have any control, he can learn where to go. He can learn not to miss the papers you've put down. You must be responsive to your puppy's needs, putting him on the papers or taking him outside when he tells you—one way or another—that it is time for a bathroom break.

Watch your puppy closely, and you'll see the look in his eye, or the special way he is walking, or the general anxiousness when he is about to relieve himself. Since he has no control, it's up to you to take him to the proper place outside or to put him on the papers.

You can look at bathroom behavior logically and determine when your puppy will need his bathroom break. Think about when you use the toilet: when you wake up from a good night's sleep or a long nap and a little while after you eat or drink. It's the same for your dog. Make sure that he can go out when he wakes up and a little while after eating. Now when you wake up, your first stop needs to be relief for the puppy. You can hold it another few minutes; he can't.

If the dog barks in the middle of the night, drag yourself out of bed and let your puppy relieve himself. It sure beats cleaning up in the morning. Wouldn't you get up to tend the needs of your baby crying in the night? Don't you sometimes have to use the bathroom in the middle of the night? Listen to what your puppy is telling you and take care of his needs.

Remember, dogs generally won't use eating or sleeping areas for toilet purposes. This is the key fact we use when house training a puppy twelve weeks or older.

Paper Training

Here's a method of training that works well with the logic and observation just described. Give the puppy a small room in the house, like the laundry room, spare bedroom or kitchen, preferably a room with a tile floor. Remember to barricade the room to confine him. Then take the puppy's room and split it in half. Put the puppy's food and bed or crate (with the door open) in one half. Then divide the other half in two. Put newspapers all over the floor in the quarter farthest from the food and bed. That's the toilet area. Put the water bowl on the edge of the paper.

Let the pup know that it's fine to mess on the papers. During the early weeks, that's the safe place he can go if you can't rush him outside.

The next step is to reduce the papered area. The pup will learn to use the papers, even though they're shrinking.

As the papers get smaller and smaller, your puppy's room will seem to him to get larger and larger. You can begin letting him into other rooms of your house or apartment little by little. The more he understands where he has to go and when, the larger the area of the house you can let him explore.

Take him outside when he needs to go, and he will begin to learn to use the outdoors. Take him to the same spot every time. Dogs like to use the same area each time, as the odors will stimulate him to action. If you let him go in only one specific area, he'll usually use that area, making outdoor cleanup an easy task.

When your dog relieves himself outdoors, tell him he's the most wonderful, best puppy that ever existed! He'll quickly associate your praise with doing his duty outside.

In just a week or two, the whole house will be his house, and his toilet will be outside where you want it!

Sample House-Training Schedule

Time	Schedule
6:00 A.M.	Wake-up/go outside.
7:00 A.M.	Breakfast/go outside.
7:30 A.M.	Walk.
12:00 P.M.	Lunch/go outside.
12:30 P.M.	Walk.
4:30 P.M.	Walk.
6:00 P.M.	Dinner/go outside.
6:30 P.M.	Walk.
9:00 P.M.	Go outside/bedtime.

Crate-Training Your Dog

The absolute best thing you can do for your dog and your own sanity is to buy your dog a crate. A crate is a large cage or kennel made from wire or plastic. Many crates look like the shipping containers airlines use to fly dogs in. For those of us who have crate-trained our dogs, we know the dogs enjoy the comfort of having their own space, and we love the security of knowing that the dog is safely out of trouble.

What are some of the benefits of crate-training your dog? How about peaceful nights, with your puppy sleeping without crying? Waking up and finding your floors without messes? Returning home and finding nothing destroyed? Driving a car without a dog squirming at your feet or under the steering wheel? Crate-training does all of this and more. It will keep your puppy happy and you and your family sane.

What kind of crate should you get? There are many varieties on the market. Some are plastic, others are wire. Some are collapsible for easy transportation, others are convertibles, good for shipping or at home, where the top comes off for easy cleaning and moving.

It's important to make sure that the crate you buy is big enough to hold your full-grown dog, even if he's just a mere pup right now. You don't want to have to buy another crate later—unless you get another dog! Also, be sure that the crate you buy fits easily in your car. There will be times when you want to take your dog in the car (such as going to the veterinarian), and the crate will keep your dog calm and secure.

In training your dog or puppy to live in the crate, you are trying to convince the dog that this is his house, his den and his special place. The crate needs to be a private space for your dog, where prying little hands (if you have any in your family) are not permitted.

The crate becomes a refuge and a mobile home for your dog, no matter where you happen to be. It makes the car, the kennel or a motel room familiar and comfortable. If your neighborhood ever has to be evacuated because of a disaster, your dog can be confined and moved without any trouble.

Dogs, like many people, like routine and their own comfy bed. The crate supplies those needs at home and elsewhere.

If the crate you buy is a used one, give it a thorough cleaning and disinfecting. Allow it to air out completely to get rid of the disinfectant smell.

If you are crate-training a puppy, put a closed cardboard box inside the crate. This will take up the excess space in the crate so it's just right and cozy for the puppy, and the puppy won't think about using part of his crate as the bathroom. As the puppy grows, replace the cardboard box with progressively smaller ones, or remove it, and you have a crate for a bigger dog!

Those crates with uncomfortable bottoms require some padding or bedding. This can be an old blanket (without fleas), or it can be a fancy, comfortable antibacterial pad available at dog shows and some pet supply stores. Whatever you choose to use, it should make a little "nest" inside the crate.

After your dog is housebroken, leave a bowl of water in the crate and be sure the water is kept fresh. Many crates have a little dish for water that hangs on the door, but this is often inadequate for the needs of a large dog left in the crate for several hours.

Introduce your dog to the crate slowly. Let him sniff the crate, walk inside and out and explore it. Put a favorite toy or treat in the crate, and tell your dog how good he is when he's inside. He'll get the idea. A treat can entice the dog inside.

Respect your dog's privacy when he's in the crate. Don't bug him and don't let the kids tease him. Keep your fingers out of the crate and just let the dog be alone in his own space.

Let your dog come out when he's good and ready. Avoid reaching in and dragging him out. Once he's used to being in the crate, close the door for a few moments while he's inside. Tell him he's a good dog and then let him come out. Try it again and he'll get used to staying in the crate with the door closed.

Don't reprimand your dog when he's in the crate, and avoid putting him in when he has misbehaved. The crate is not a jail or place of punishment. A crate is not a disciplinary device. It is the dog's bedroom, and should represent a happy place to your dog.

Some people feed the dog in the crate. This is good, as it reinforces the crate as a happy place where many of the dog's needs are met. It also prevents your dog from sneaking food from another pet's bowl.

If begging at the table is a problem, the crate can be a way to encourage the dog to eat his dinner while you are enjoying yours.

A dog usually won't relieve himself where he sleeps, unless he is poorly trained, desperate or has a medical problem. You can use this knowledge, along with the crate, to train your dog to relieve himself where and when you want. The dog won't eliminate in the crate, unless it's too big for him. He'll wait until he's out of the crate, and that's when you can rush him outside to "the spot." Again, remember that dogs need to go at particular times: first thing in the morning, shortly after sunrise (for most puppies), when they wake up from a nap, when you get back after the dog has been left alone and right after meals. The dog also needs to go just before you go to bed at night and whenever he lets you know with a cry, a bark or that certain look in his eyes.

Of course, you wouldn't start off your dog with four hours in the crate. Start with just a few minutes in the crate, followed by play-time. Every day, increase the amount of time he is left alone in his crate. In just a few weeks, your dog will be content to stay in the crate while you are out.

When crate-training puppies, do not close the door until the puppy has not urinated or defecated during the night. When the puppy can control his eliminations through the night, then you can begin to close the door. If you close the door before he can control his elimination, you'll be telling him it's okay to use the crate as a bathroom.

It is permissible to correct your dog if he whines, barks or howls because he doesn't want to be in the crate and not because he has to go to the bathroom. You can tap on the front door of the crate and say, "No, quiet"; cover the crate with a towel; tell him to be quiet and ignore him; or spray him with a squirt bottle full of water, repeating, "No, quiet." He'll settle down shortly.

If your puppy is barking because he doesn't want to be in the crate, do not let him out, as this will reinforce the behavior of barking. He'll learn that you will let him out of the crate every time he barks, and that is the wrong lesson. He must learn to stay in the crate without barking to be released. You, on the other hand, must learn to distinguish the difference between the bark your dog gives to tell you it's time to get outside to relieve himself and the bark he gives because he doesn't want to be in the crate.

Warning: To avoid strangulation, never leave your puppy or dog confined in his crate wearing a training collar, choke chain or nylon slip collar!

Early Basic Training II

An untrained dog rules the house. He will get away with everything he can. Dogs need a leader within their human pack, just as they need a canine pack leader in the wild. If the dog is not provided with a leader, he will fill the vacuum himself. You and your family will become the subordinates, instead of the leaders. Training establishes you as the leader. Continued training throughout the dog's life gets you reelected to your leadership position.

The first purpose of training is to establish who is the leader and who is the follower. You, as the leader, must teach the dog good manners and acceptable behavior, reinforce good behavior and correct undesirable behavior.

Some dogs will assume the leadership role if given a chance. Watch your dog's body language and behaviors to see if he is trying to become the leader of the house. There is nothing worse than having your dog be the leader.

Biting and Chewing on People

Biting or mouthing your hands or clothing should never be allowed. This behavior should be nipped in the bud the minute it starts. It's easy to communicate this to your puppy. Use his previous experiences with littermates to teach him what you want him to do.

A puppy who gets bitten by a brother or sister yelps. If he annoys his mother, he gets a low growl. Use these same lessons to teach your dog. If your puppy is mouthing on you, putting his mouth around your hand or finger, let out a high-pitched "Ouch!" followed by a firm "*No! Bad dog!*" in a low voice. The puppy will equate this to his experiences with siblings and mother and stop.

If the puppy does not respond to the ouch, gently shake him by the scruff of the neck (not hard, but just enough for him to know you mean business) and say, "*No!*" The next level of correction is to roll the puppy over on his back (belly exposed), look him straight in his eyes, gently place your hand around his throat and say, "*No!*" These corrections also tie into what momma dog did with her puppies.

Remember, once the undesired behavior has stopped, you must reward the dog, saying in a happy voice, "Good dog!" This method of correction can also be used to stop other unwanted activities.

Warning Signs of a Biting Dog

"Out of the blue, my dog bit me!" How many times have dog trainers heard that?

Before a biting incident, there are almost always warning signs . . . but the owner didn't notice them. Does your dog insist on being first out the door? Will he defend his food dish like a pirate's treasure? Does he growl if you try to take away a bone or a toy? Is he afraid of being touched and uncomfortable around strange people or objects?

These are all warning signs that your dog has behavioral problems. He finds certain situations very stressful, and may react by biting. Unless you change the behavior of your dog, relieve his fear and train him to be a good canine citizen, you're likely to get a nasty bite, or at least a good nip.

You must head off the biting situation before it happens. Expose your puppy to other animals and people at an early age. Enroll him in a "puppy kindergarten class" given by a local training club or a trainer. (This is important for every dog.) Help the puppy become accustomed to new situations and gain confidence around other dogs and people. The puppy must learn which behaviors are acceptable and appropriate in a given situation.

The dominant dog who insists on being first out the door and the aggressive dog who growls over possessions or food must be retrained. Professional help is called for, especially if you have an older dog with a major dominance problem or a fearful dog. (Many people don't realize that dogs who are afraid are quick to bite.) Contact your veterinarian for advice. He may recommend an animal behaviorist or trainer who can help you solve these behavior problems.

Teething and Chewing

All dogs need to chew on things. It massages the gums, which is important for their dental health. However, you should be in control of what is chewed by replacing an undesired behavior with one that is desirable. If your puppy is chewing on your favorite pair of shoes, say the command "No!" and give the dog an object he can safely chew on, such as a commercially available biscuit or a safe dog toy.

Tooth Loss

Between the ages of four and five months, your puppy will start getting his adult teeth. Like a baby, your puppy will be teething, encountering discomfort as the new teeth come in. He will want to chew on anything he can get his mouth around: books, furniture and you.

As new teeth come in, old teeth fall out. You may find teeth around the house or one may be left dangling by the root. If a baby tooth doesn't want to drop away, it can cause permanent misalignment of the other teeth. You can help the situation along by checking your puppy's mouth frequently during this time and providing plenty of sturdy toys to chew on. If a tooth seems stuck, have your veterinarian take care of it. Don't try to pull it yourself.

Like a teething baby, your puppy might get cranky. Something cool like an ice cube can help soothe sore gums. A little extra patience and loving care will get your puppy through this time of discomfort.

Collar and Leash

A well-trained dog is a joy to his owner and everyone he comes in contact with over his lifetime. But you must start his training early or he may acquire bad habits that will haunt you forever.

Basic training begins when your puppy comes home, but formal training starts with learning to wear a collar and accepting a leash. It's a hard transition, from total freedom to a controlled learning situation in a short time. Diligence, consistency, repetition, patience and love combine to make training a simple yet rewarding task. Remember, a puppy has a short attention span. Work quickly, while he is interested!

Your dog loves you, respects you and will do anything to please you. You are responsible for communicating what you want in a clear and understandable (to him!) manner. The collar and the leash are the tools necessary to open the lines of communication.

Your puppy's first collar should be lightweight, adjustable and have a buckle. It can be either nylon or leather. Nylon is usually less expensive. As your puppy grows, you will buy several collars, especially if he's one of the larger breeds!

Buy a collar that fits your puppy now. It should fit snugly, much like your own belt. Don't buy one that's too big with the idea he will grow into it! A loose collar can be dangerous, catching onto fences and other objects.

Begin with the thinnest, lightest collar and let your puppy get used to the idea of wearing it. Let him wear it for a week or two. He'll probably be totally annoyed by it and try to scratch it off, but he'll get used to it. Once he's stopped scratching and is used to the idea of wearing a collar, it's time to graduate to a more durable, more formal collar with a loop for attaching a leash.

Your first leash should be at least six feet long with a small swivel snap. The length of the leash is important, as you need a long leash for training classes. Introduce the leash to your puppy, but remember, it's not a toy for him to play with but a teaching aid to learn with.

Snap the leash on the collar and allow your puppy to get accustomed to the idea of the leash. You can let him wander around in the house, dragging the leash until he gets used to it. Watch the puppy to make sure he doesn't get tangled. When he has come to accept the leash, take him outside for fun and adventure.

Help your dog to always associate the leash with a fun time of learning and exploring—not simply walking.

If your puppy is reserved or timid, you'll need to offer reassurance and coaxing. Take him by the leash and encourage him to explore. If your puppy is self-confident he'll want to lead you around. Your job is to start teaching him that you are the leader.

Dog ID

One of the most important things you can do to safeguard your pets is make sure that they have identification. Any dog can get lost or stolen. There are a number of ways to ensure that anyone who finds your dog will also be able to find you. The most common type of ID is a dog tag. Pet stores and veterinarians usually have forms that you can use to mail away for these tags, which should include your name and phone numbers—home and work. And when your dog gets his rabies vaccination, your veterinarian will give you a tag that can be traced back to his or her office. However, because these tags are removable, they are not failsafe. Other options to consider include tattoos and microchips. Microchips are programmed with the same information that would appear on a dog tag and surgically implanted under your dog's skin. These two forms of ID are invaluable in cases where you need to be able to prove that you own the animal in question.

5

The Responsible Dog Owner

My dogs are raised knowing the world revolves around their happiness and well being . . . But it's important to realize not everyone feels the same way about your dog as you do. Taking other people's concerns, feelings and fears about dogs into account is a big part of responsible pet ownership.

JOAN EMBERY

~

MANY DOG OWNERS SAY, "LOVE ME, LOVE MY DOG." UNFORTUnately, not all people love dogs the way you do.

One way to help people love your dog is to make sure he is trained and well mannered. The time you spend training your dog will be returned to you with love, companionship and a worry-free environment. You'll be able to spend more time with your dog and less time fighting with your neighbors over your dog's behavior.

You, Your Dog and the Law

Each state, town, community, park and beach in the United States has its own regulations. Generally, the law requires a dog to be licensed and to have proof of a rabies vaccination that is current. Usually, your dog must be leashed when off your property, and you must clean up after your dog if he eliminates on public property. Many cities also have nuisance ordinances that prohibit dogs from barking after 10 P.M. and before 7 A.M. Quite a few states require a recent health certificate before you transport your dog in from another state.

Check state and local laws in your area before you bring your puppy home. Many towns now have limitations on the total number of animals you may have in your household. Other cities have regulations regarding the breeding of dogs within the city limits.

Where do you start finding out about local laws? Look in the telephone book under Government Services, local or state, for licenses and permits, or under the Department of Agriculture heading.

For local laws regarding the number of dogs you may own or the breeding of dogs, call your town supervisor or city hall and ask them for a copy of the dog laws. You can also try looking up the information under zoning laws.

Walking Your Dog

All dogs need daily exercise. It's best to have a fenced yard or enclosure so he can have the freedom to play without becoming a traffic hazard or a nuisance to the neighborhood. If you can't afford to have your yard fenced then you should walk your dog daily on a leash.

A daily walk can be a treat for both your dog and you, especially if you have trained your dog to walk quietly on a loose lead. Teaching your dog to walk at your left side (heeling) helps you control your dog, keeps him from jumping up on people, frightening or possibly injuring passersby, and prevents him from interfering with other dogs.

Curbing Your Dog

On walks, allow your dog to poop only near the curb, next to the street . . . and clean it up!

When the dog is about to relieve himself, guide him toward the curb. This will soon become a habit for both of you. Many cities now have laws concerning where your dog is permitted to defecate and removal requirements. Some cities have laws declaring the grassy strip between the sidewalk and the street public property. The city controls this area and will fine owners should they not remove their dogs' feces.

Many dogwalkers take along sandwich bags to tidily pick up after their pooch. To keep the yard clean, use a pooper scooper—a shovel and scoop device made especially for picking up dog droppings without having to bend over. The accumulation of dog feces in a yard attracts flies and causes odor problems and can lead to disease spreading between dogs. Most cities have health code regulations for the removal of dog excrement.

Being responsible means keeping your dog from urinating on the neighbors' plantings, cleaning up when your dog defecates, walking your dog regularly and having a fenced yard to prevent the dog from roaming about the neighborhood.

In many cities, a dog running at large is defined as a dangerous dog. The owner is subject to stiff penalties, ranging from as little as $25 to as much as $500, with increasing penalties for each incident.

Fences, Feces and Yard Manners

You can teach your dog to relieve himself in a specific area of your yard. You can also teach him the boundary of your yard.

Start training your dog when he is a puppy. Place some of his feces in the area you want him to use and take him to this spot each time he has to relieve himself. Praise him for his actions. But remember you must clean this area regularly. No dog likes to have to step around or in his own droppings.

Spray dog repellent on other locations to inhibit him from wandering there. By reinforcing this use of the specific area and teaching him which areas are off limits, you and your neighbors will remain friendly, as your dog will stay where he belongs.

Keep Your Dog in the Yard

If you don't walk your dog on a leash, fence your yard. Even if a portion of yard is fenced into a dog run, you'll find that most of your neighbor problems can be eliminated.

You could confine your dog to the yard with a swivel stake and chain, but this is not recommended. The chain does not prevent the neighborhood kids from coming over and teasing the dog. Also, the dog may become entangled in the chain and injure himself. And, a dog restricted to a chain can break loose, running like the wind to enjoy his freedom. Good luck catching the newly freed dog!

A cable and trolley system is better than being chained and is relatively inexpensive—but it's not recommended either. You loop the cable around a tree or a pole and string it eight to ten feet off the ground. One end of the trolley leash is attached to the cable and the other end to the dog's collar. The trolley leash is made out of the same wire cable and is coated with plastic. The trolley leash should be long enough to allow the dog to lie down comfortably without getting tangled. There are better alternatives than a trolley system—such as a fenced run.

Another alternative is the Invisible Fence® or the Radio Fence®. These send radio signals from a wire buried a few inches below the surface to an alert device on your dog's collar. The dog learns to stay within the boundary marked by the radio wire. This works well at keeping dogs in but does nothing to keep other dogs (and children) out. And there are times when a dog will put up with the pain of crossing the boundary to chase a cat or rabbit. Then the dog can't get back across the boundary without human help.

When your dog is outside, always make sure there is plenty of shade for him to sleep in and water to drink.

No matter what you use to contain your dog outside, never leave the dog outside when you are not home. Too many things can happen.

A Barking Dog Is a Nuisance!

No one enjoys a barking dog, and this bad habit should be nipped in the bud. Furthermore, it is illegal in many areas. A dog should bark only when you want him to.

Here's what to do if your dog is in a fenced backyard and barks constantly. First, tell the dog to *"be quiet!"* Say it in a firm voice.

Is the dog ignoring you? Try the "shake can." Take an empty soda can and put two or three pennies in it. Tape the hole. Throw the can so that it will drop near the dog. The can will make lots of noise when it hits the ground and rolls away. Now that you have your dog's full attention, give the command "be quiet!"

Another alternative will work if your dog has already had basic obedience training. Just put him in a down-stay position. Dogs cannot bark easily when they are lying down.

Once the dog has settled down, reward him with a happy "good dog."

Female Dogs in Heat and the Unneutered Male

What would you do with any puppies your female dog produced? (Hint: Giving them away to friends is not an acceptable answer, unless you have quite a few dog-loving friends who happen to want another dog.) The sad fact is that too many "accidental" puppies end up at the shelter, where they will be kept for up to five days. After that, they will be euthanized. Due to the great demand for shelter space, that is the reality. Most shelters have to euthanize unadopted animals after three to five days, and the odds of being adopted just aren't that great.

Your female dog comes into heat twice a year which will last for about a month each time. During this time, all the unaltered male dogs in the surrounding area will be calling on her to mate. Generally, the male dogs in the neighborhood will whine, bark and howl in your yard out of frustration. Male dogs may set up house on your steps to get to your female. Males will go to great lengths to gain access to a female in heat. A female dog in heat with male dogs-running at large is a nuisance and very annoying to you and your neighbors.

An unspayed female in heat needs to be confined to prevent an unplanned breeding. Some people choose to board their female at the veterinarian's office or local boarding kennel for the month. Otherwise, you'll have to take special precautions with her. Walk her outside only to relieve herself, always on a leash. Watch her every movement outdoors, keeping males away. Be prepared to clean up spots of blood around the house, as she may drip. Keep her off the furniture unless you want to clean up bloodstains. Don't take her to a public park. Many states and cities require the confinement of females in heat. The state of Pennsylvania and the city of Germantown, Tennessee, are two examples.

The solution to all this is simple. Spay your female dog, neuter your male dog.

Spaying and Neutering

All dogs not intended for shows or breeding should be spayed or neutered! Spaying and neutering are relatively simple procedures. Your veterinarian can tell you about them, and when they should be done. It is generally recommended that you spay and neuter your dogs before they are six months old.

Studies have shown that dogs who have been spayed or neutered are less susceptible to a whole range of diseases. These operations can help your dog live a healthier, longer life.

People often manage to come up with an excuse for not spaying or neutering their dog. The only good excuse for not doing it is if your dog is such a terrific specimen that you will make the commitment of time and money needed to show the dog for his or her Conformation. At that point, you can consider breeding the dog.

Here are the common excuses, and why they are just plain silly:

"We want to have another dog just like him." The odds of this happening are a thousand to one. Breeding two purebred dogs of the same breed and similar genetic backgrounds rarely results in a puppy exactly like either one of the parents. With mixed breeds, it is virtually impossible. Enjoy your great dog and cherish the time you have with him. Don't try to clone him. Science hasn't perfected that technique yet.

"My dog will get fat and lazy if it is spayed or neutered." This only happens when dogs are overfed and under-exercised. You may have to cut back on the food intake and increase the amount of exercise your dog gets, but not all dogs who are spayed get fat.

"We can sell puppies and make money." Breeding is an extremely difficult business. It's tough to break even, let alone make money. To do it right, you pay for the stud (a male for hire), vaccinations, dewormings and other veterinary fees, plus the cost of good puppy food. This is all costly.

"My dog's personality will change." Any change will be for the better. Altering reduces aggression toward other dogs, and cuts the desire to wander. If your dog is neutered at six months of age, there will be no noticeable change in personality.

"My children should witness the miracle of birth." Dogs often wait until the middle of the night to have their puppies. The kids might sleep through it. What if the mother dies or the puppies are born dead? How will this affect your children? Clearly, there are better ways to show the children the miracle of birth.

Three More Good Reasons to Spay/Neuter

• **Spaying or neutering increases your dog's chances for a longer, healthier life.** If your female is spayed early (age six months), the chances of developing breast cancer are greatly reduced. Uterine infections, along with uterine or ovarian cancers, are no longer possibilities. Neutering your male may eliminate prostate problems and, of course, eliminate testicular tumors. It also decreases the risk of perianal tumors, often seen in older, unaltered dogs.

• **Your male dog will be a better family pet.** Males neutered early in life are less aggressive toward other dogs. They aren't distracted by neighborhood females in heat and are, therefore, easier to train.

• **Your female dog will always be ready for performance events.** Spayed females and neutered males are eligible to enter obedience trials, field trials, hunting tests, and sighthound lure coursing trials. If your female comes in heat, you are sidelined for at least three weeks, twice a year.

The Surgical Procedure

Thousands of dogs are spayed or neutered every day. Both operations are low-risk procedures, usually without complications. Typical spay and neuter procedures are discussed below. *Please consult your veterinarian because these surgical procedures may vary.*

Normally, your veterinarian will instruct you to withhold food and water from your dog for twelve hours or overnight before the operation. Immediately prior to surgery, your dog will be given preanesthetic agents and injected with a light anesthetic. Next, a tube attached to a tank of anesthetic gas is inserted into the trachea. This procedure usually maintains the amount of anesthesia needed during surgery. When your dog is asleep, the veterinary technician will shave the operation site and cleanse the skin with an antiseptic scrub to ensure that the skin is free of bacteria. Throughout the surgery, your dog will be closely monitored.

Neutering your male dog is fairly simple. An incision is made in front of the scrotum, the blood vessels leading to the testicles are clamped and tied, and the testicles are removed. The incision is then closed with sutures. Although your dog may be awake in a few hours, he may be kept in the veterinary clinic overnight.

Spaying your female dog is more complicated. An incision is made in the abdomen and the vessels that supply blood to the uterus and ovaries are clamped and tied. The uterus and ovaries are then removed. After the veterinarian makes sure that there is no bleeding, the incision is closed with multiple layers of sutures or staples. Following the operation, your dog will probably remain in the hospital at least overnight.

When your female comes home, she should be confined to the house for a few days and always walked on a leash. Your biggest problem with a newly spayed female is keeping her quiet. Make sure she does not jump or bite at her sutures.

In eight to ten days, the incision will heal and the sutures or staples will be removed by your veterinarian, unless they are self-dissolving.

When Service People Come

Let your dog get acquainted with the mail carrier, meter reader, garbage collector, UPS person and the paper carrier. Tell them your dog's name and give them a treat to give to your dog. After a few times, the dog will greet them as friends.

If you fence your yard, make sure the service people have access to the items they need—they don't like to go into a fenced yard with dogs. They don't know your dog and your dog may not allow them to enter the yard. If your dog perceives a service person as an intruder he may try to bite. Be considerate of the people who service you on a regular basis.

What to Do If Your Dog Is Missing

One of the scariest times of a dog owner's life is when the dog is missing. Did somebody steal the dog? It happens. More likely, though, the dog made an escape and is enjoying an adventure in the neighborhood.

When dogs get lost, they have a bad habit of getting *really* lost. They go off chasing a cat and suddenly end up in unfamiliar territory . . . lost. They don't know their way home.

If your dog is missing, it is critical to act quickly. Check the immediate area thoroughly, including the house, the yard, the car and the garage. Check with your family—someone may have taken the dog with him or her. If you have a small dog, look under the bed and behind closed doors.

Next, call the local humane society, dog pound, animal shelters, animal control department and police department. Notify them, and see if anyone has called about a strange dog wandering around. Tell them whether he was wearing a collar with identification. Give a general description.

Call your veterinarian. Many rabies tags have the veterinarian's name and number, and a person finding the dog will call there first. Keep the license number on file.

The next step is to put the search into high gear. Make a flyer and distribute it everywhere. Photocopy a good photo of your dog onto it. Leave flyers with all the veterinarians in the area, the police and fire departments, animal control and the post office. Give one to your mail carrier, milkman, fuel delivery man and UPS driver. Post it at shelters, pounds, humane societies, the local shopping center and around the neighborhood.

Call local radio stations—many make lost and found pet announcements. Put an ad in the lost pet section of the classifieds in all of the newspapers and shopper's guides in your town and in surrounding towns.

If your utility company has a local office, give them a copy of the flyer, too. Meter readers see plenty of dogs.

Drop the flyer off at the nearby school and give one to the school bus driver who covers your area. Leave flyers with nearby gas stations, convenience stores, fast food restaurants, community centers and even town hall. The more people you have looking for your dog—or aware he is missing—the more likely someone will see him.

Prepare a written description of the dog and include a photograph. Include the dog's name, sex and age, plus the breed, size, weight and color. Add details such as the dog's tail length and style and type of fur.

Remember when giving these descriptions that most people know little about dogs. Use points of reference for average people, not dog people. If you say your dog is medium size, medium is relative. A boxer may be medium size compared to a great dane, but huge compared to a toy poodle. Again, give a reference point such as "the dog is about eighteen inches tall." Describe your dog as though the reader knows nothing about dogs!

Be sure to include your name and phone numbers, both home and work, and the area in which your dog was last seen. Never include any reference to the dog's monetary value. Some dogs are stolen and held for ransom. If you decide to give a reward do not state the amount. State "a reward is offered for information leading to the return of this dog."

Be sure to check the newspapers daily under the Found Pet section. Remember, once the flyers have been distributed someone must stay by the phone unless you have an answering machine.

The American Humane Association and Sprint have a national telephone line to match lost pets with found ones. Call (900) 535-1515 to report your pet lost. (It costs $1.95 a minute and takes about four minutes.) Call (800) 755-8111 to report a found pet. (It's free.) The system allows for a detailed description of the pet, including zip code where the pet was lost or found. The pet owner can call and check to see if any pets matching the description have been found. Updates like this take about a minute or the system will call you automatically when a match is made.

How Much Ransom Is *Your* Dog Worth?

What happens when the person who finds a lost dog wants to make some money on the reward? In South Carolina, he might end up in jail.

Here's how the story went:

Sheila Jennings of Spartanburg, South Carolina, lost her five-year-old Yorkie on June 8. Three days later, Ronnie White, eighteen, called her and told her he had Bentley and would return him for the $50 reward offered on Sheila's flyers. But he never brought the dog.

Sheila then received two phone calls in one day from a woman who said she had the dog and the $50 reward was not enough. A man came on the line during one phone call to demand $200. Even though Sheila agreed to the price, Bentley still didn't find his way home. That same day the woman called Sheila a third time, saying that her son had grown very attached to the dog.

Sheila offered the dognappers one of the puppies the next time she bred Bentley. But they just weren't interested.

Two days later, a relative of one of the captors saw a TV news report and convinced them to return the dog. The captors told Sheila to meet them at a local gas station.

That night the meeting was held. The dog was returned unharmed, and two teenaged couples were arrested and charged with conspiracy to commit extortion. In South Carolina, that carries a maximum penalty of five years in prison or as much as a $5,000 fine.

Death of the Family Pet

It's a sad reality but pets usually don't live as long as their masters. As someone who has owned dogs all of my life, I've experienced the death of several pets. Most recently, our black lab Drifter passed away after being with us nearly thirteen years. This loss was particularly devastating because Drifter was a sick stray who literally wound up on our door step and who we nursed from illness to health. Over the years we went through quite a lot with Drifter, and when she died, it felt like we had lost a part of ourselves. Drifter was so involved in our lives—on the ranch, traveling around the country, at horse shows. While no animal will ever be able to replace her, we believe that each pet adds their own special something to your life, a unique set of shared experiences and memories, which is the reason we will always be dog owners.

JOAN EMBERY

~

The death of the family dog is like the loss of a member of the family. There are five steps in the grieving process that most people go through. Although not everyone goes through all of the stages, and each one can last anywhere from minutes to days, understanding the process will help you to cope with the loss of your pet.

The first stage is **DENIAL.** Denial buffers our feelings against a sharp emotional blow. Your mind tries to deny that the pet actually is dying or has died. During this time, don't be surprised if you keep expecting to see or hear your dog. This is a normal reaction to a major change.

The second stage is called **"MAKING THE BARGAIN."** People often will bargain with God: "If you bring Fido back, I'll never forget to give him his treats, or let him loose again, etc."

The third stage is **ANGER** and **RAGE.** Typically, anger is aimed at the person closest to the death, like your veterinarian. This is the time when you are most likely to say things you'll regret later—so recognizing this state of grief is very important.

Eventually, anger is directed inward and is replaced by **GUILT:** "If only I hadn't let the dog out of my sight." This stage can be especially difficult for very young children whose thought processes make it natural for them to assume that they are somehow responsible for everything that happens.

The last stage is **GRIEF.** You have finally accepted that the dog is gone. Your feelings of anger and guilt have eased. And while this is the time that you need support from your family and friends, not everyone will understand how deeply some of us are affected by the loss of an animal. Recognizing this will make it easier to deal with people who say:"It was only a dog . . ."

If you have a friend who has lost a pet, realize the stages they are going through and comfort them when they need you. If you are having trouble coping with the loss of a pet, check with your veterinarian or telephone crisis line. Many cities now have support groups for people who have lost their pets.

The most satisfying way to ease the grief associated with losing a beloved pet is to get another one. Many people resist this, feeling that would be somehow disloyal to the dog that has died.

Since dogs don't live nearly as long as humans, dealing with the death of a pet is a hard reality of dog ownership. Whatever the reason for your dog's death—old age, disease, or even an accident—you shouldn't deny yourself the pleasure of having a relationship with a dog, or let your loving home go to waste. No dog can replace the one you lost. But most of us have room in our hearts to love more than one dog, and love them each for their own unique qualities.

6

Training Your Dog

TRAINING IS DEFINED AS A CHANGE IN BEHAVIOR. DOG TRAIN-
ing is the change in a dog's behavior as a result of the training
process. We train our dogs to discourage them from engaging in
activities we find objectionable. We also train our dogs to encourage
them to perform in a manner we would find acceptable. Dogs, like
people, have limitations on what they can learn. Dogs also differ
on how they can be taught; this difference is due to language. The
written and spoken word is an expression of human thought and is
the means by which people communicate with one another. Dogs
cannot understand the written word or complex sentences. To communicate with your dog effectively you must use sentences shortened
to a single word or phrase—called a *command*. This is the greatest
distinction between how dogs and people can be taught.

To be successful at training your dog you must teach the dog to
respond to a single word or command. To be an effective
dog trainer you should be familiar with learning theories and dog
training techniques. Many different training methods have proven
successful and are included in this book.

Conditioning Theories

The learning theories applicable to dog training are a derivation of the two major themes of conditioning: instrumental conditioning and classical conditioning. Conditioning is the process whereby a dog associates a specific task with a command, with the prospect of positive reinforcement.

Classical conditioning theories are primarily derived from the work of Ivan Petrovich Pavlov (1849–1936). Pavlov believed that stimuli in the environment caused the individual's behavior, insofar as such behavior is an existing reflex. To Pavlov, learning occurred as a result of the stimuli being paired with the reflex. In dog training, the function of classical conditioning is to form associations between a particular task and a specific command. All dogs can sit by their own volition, but in the process of conditioning this task becomes associated with an appropriate command. Classically conditioned behaviors, such as sitting on command, depend on the already existing sit reflex that can be elicited by a preceding stimulus, like the command "sit!"

Instrumental conditioning theories of learning are derived primarily from the work of Edward L. Thorndike (1874–1949). He theorized that individuals learn to do things—respondent behaviors—that produce pleasant effects and learn to avoid those activities that produce unpleasant effects. Thorndike found that instrumental conditioning is important for regulating the frequency of any given task or behavior. The frequency of the respondent behavior is dependent upon the frequency of the eliciting stimulus. Thorndike discovered that a positive stimulus will increase the frequency of the behavior and a negative stimulus will decrease the frequency of the behavior.

Classical and instrumental conditioning techniques are both important for dog training. The principles of instrumental conditioning are useful for regulating the frequency of any given task. Whereas classical conditioning techniques help form associations between a particular task and a relevant command. All dogs can sit, lie down, come, walk and stay of their own volition. The process of training associates these tasks with specific commands, so the dog's behavior may be controlled by you.

Learning Theories

All training programs are based on the pairing of conduct with pleasure or displeasure. To get your dog to perform a given task, you must make the task tempting and pleasant. Positive reinforcement is one of the simplest forms of reward. In most cases it is limited to verbal praise. Simple phrases such as "good boy," "that 'a girl" or "ooooh, what a wonderful puppy" tell the dog to keep doing what he is doing. In dog training, verbal positive reinforcement or food rewards are used to encourage a dog to perform a task, and a correction or reprimand is used to discourage a particular activity.

It is said that practice makes perfect. The more an individual practices a task or makes the same behavioral response in a given situation, the more likely that particular task or response will be made the next time the same situation is encountered.

This concept can be applied for improving a dog's performance by regulating when you reward the dog's behavior. For example, as the dog demonstrates he has learned the task, positive reinforcements should then be given only when the task was performed better than on a previous trial; thus, the task is likely to be improved.

This is also an important concept to help you understand how a dog's habits are formed and established. For example, if a dog is given food while begging at the dinner table, each time you give the dog food while he begs at the table increases the likelihood that the dog will beg at subsequent mealtimes. Knowing this concept will help you understand that the formation of the dog's behavior was directly proportional to the rate at which you fed the dog from the table and that the establishment of the dog's behavior was reinforced each time you gave the dog food while the dog begged at the table.

This will also help you understand the importance of your actions for improving your dog's behavior. Continuing from the example above, the dog, having now been conditioned to respond to the stimulus of receiving food while begging at the table, may generalize this behavior to other similar, yet inappropriate stimuli, such as grabbing food out of your hand when you are not sitting at the table. At first, the dog's response to the food in your hand will not be as consistent as when he comes to the table during each mealtime. If you allow the begging at the table to continue, you will be reinforcing the second behavior—snatching food from your hand—and a new habit will be established. If you correct the dog for inappropriately grabbing food from your hand, the dog will learn to discriminate between the two situations. The responses that are not reinforced will disappear and the encouraged behaviors will be preserved.

Another fact we must take into consideration when we train our dogs is their disposition. You cannot make generalized statements about how a dog will react in any given situation without first considering the dog's temperament or disposition. An individual dog's motivation, drive and determination to make a given response will influence what response is made and when it is made. The importance of recognizing the individual difference seen in dogs should not be overlooked. In dog training classes, as with a classroom full of fifth graders, you have a variety of dispositions: your class clowns, dominant bullies, shy wallflowers, oversensitive dogs and independent dogs. To be successful at training your dog you should know and understand your dog's disposition.

Dog Dispositions

A **shy or nervous dog** is insecure and fearful of the outside world. He will normally walk around in a crouched manner with his tail tucked between his legs. He may also be oversensitive to noise and hand movements. This dog needs to be handled gently with lots of praise for encouragement and reassurance. Training will help this dog gain confidence. You must be consistent and patient. A shy dog may require many repetitions of the same exercise before he feels secure enough to try it on his own. You must understand the delicate balance between giving too much praise and not enough. Too much praise or coddling the dog will reinforce the wallflower behavior. Insufficient praise will keep the dog from gaining the confidence he needs to feel secure about the outside world. Shy or nervous dogs typically do not need to be corrected or reprimanded for making a mistake. You should physically place or guide the dog into the proper position.

The **oversensitive dog** needs to be handled in much the same manner; he too needs reassurance and confidence. The difference between the oversensitive dog and the shy dog is that the oversensitive dog is not fearful of the outside environment. The oversensitive dog is reluctant to do anything wrong that may cause you to become upset with him. Training the oversensitive dog is limited to voice inflections, happy tone of voice for praise and a scornful low voice for reprimands. Should the dog make a mistake or not perform the task correctly he should not be punished.

The **dominant dog** usually recognizes his own physical strength and power. If given the opportunity, he will use it. The dominant dog also respects authority, provided you take the leadership role. You must be firm, assertive and decisive in the dog's training exercises, otherwise the dominant dog will overpower you. Commands should be given in a firm voice. Praise should be limited to one word and given only for a job well done. This dog can handle a reprimand but it must be done in an authoritative manner. The dog should not perceive the reprimand or correction as a threat. He should view the correction as subordination to the leadership role of the student, much like the relationship that exists between the boot camp sergeant and the inductee. The reprimand or correction is conducted through the leash and the actions of the dog's collar. The dominant dog may try to challenge your authority. You should be aware of this fact. It is your job as the trainer to maintain a leadership role and be extremely decisive when giving commands and praise.

The **class clown** is a dog who is having so much fun that he does not want to be serious about anything. The class clown has a limited attention span. You should not allow the dog to anticipate your next move. You have to keep the dog off guard, so that he will have to pay attention. This type of dog needs little encouragement. He is rather excitable. All praise to the class-clown dog should be given in a nonchalant manner. If you use exuberant praise, as with the shy dog, the class clown will wag his tail so hard his whole body will wiggle and he will forget the command given to him. The hardest aspect of training the class clown is to remind yourself to be firm and not to laugh at your dog's antics. It is important when dealing with the class clown that his spirit remain intact. If you are too harsh with a class clown he will sulk and refuse to work.

The **independent dog** is lethargic and sees you as a source for room and board only. He usually does not care about what is taking place in his environment unless it directly concerns him or his desires. His behavior gives you the impression of nonchalance: "Who cares, so what, big deal, when I'm good and ready to perform I will." This dog needs lots of attention to feel that what he is doing is fun and beneficial to him. You need to raise this dog's spirits. Exuberant praise and animated actions are the key to train this type of dog successfully. Typically, this dog does not need to be reprimanded because he will not take the initiative to do anything on his own that would lead him to make a mistake. Your objective is to get the dog to perform a given task, regardless of how it is performed. Scheduling when praise is given will improve how the task is performed.

Punishment such as hitting, screaming, shouting or berating a dog is totally unnecessary and useless. This is true for training all dogs. A dog should never be physically punished or reprimanded when he is trying to learn what it is you want him to do. Once the dog has demonstrated that he understands what he is to do, then, and only then, can he be corrected for his error. Correcting a dog for an error is not the same as punishment. A simple correction can take the form of a firm verbal command such as "no!" The correction will be meaningless to the dog if it is not done at the precise moment the error is occurring. It is your job as the trainer to determine if the dog is confused or knowledgeable.

Dog Training

Sometimes you can train a dog to do unusual things. Such was the case when we taught Traveler how to lead a horse. It started when she was a puppy and would grab the horse's lead rope with her mouth and pull. As time went on, we helped her "train" the horse to follow her from the barn into the trailer and back. It is quite amusing to see Traveler walking down the barn aisle with a horse in tow.

JOAN EMBERY

Dogs, like people, have individual differences, and you need to take these differences into consideration. The dispositions, attitudes and learning curve of your dog will influence what type of learning environment is needed and which training technique to use. Dogs are very adaptable and easily learn what we want to teach them. The key is to communicate with them in a manner they will understand. This is true whether you have a puppy or an older dog. Both will learn equally well, given the opportunity. You, as the dog's trainer, should realize not all dogs will learn the desired training objective using the same training technique. For this reason, several methods have been included in the text. You will find one method works well with one type of dog, while it may be useless with another.

To have a better understanding of how these methods are employed, a discussion of the proper training equipment is necessary.

Training Equipment

The use of proper training equipment is extremely important. Effective communication with your dog cannot take place if the wrong training equipment is used. The equipment common to all training programs is the training collar and leash.

The best training collar is the welded metal chain-link variety, or it can be constructed of rolled nylon with metal rings at each end (see diagram 1). Slip the chain through one of the rings so the collar forms a loop, with the chain sliding through one ring and the other ring left for attachment to the leash (see diagram 2). This training collar has been found to be the most effective one to control the dog during training. It allows the dog owner to exert as little or as much control as needed. When you want to get your dog's attention or urge him into a desired position or some direction, give a light, quick jerk on the leash that *momentarily* tightens the collar around the dog's neck. Then release the pressure *instantly*. At this point, the correction will have been made (see diagram 3).

To achieve this effect, put the collar on the dog with the loose ring at the right of the dog's neck, with the chain attached to it coming over the neck and through the holding ring, rather than

Diagram 1
Training Collar

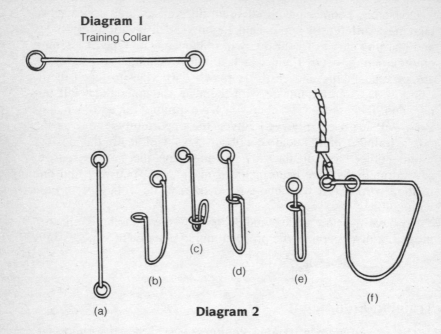

(a)

(b)

(c)

(d)

(e)

(f)

Diagram 2

under the neck (see diagram 4). It seems like a small point, but as the dog is at your left during most of training, this arrangement is what makes the collar effective. It allows the collar to loosen instantly when you have finished the quick jerk on the leash.

The proper training leash is made of leather or webbing and should be six feet long and one half inch to one inch wide. Your right hand always holds the loop of the leash (see diagram 5). There are, however, four different positions for your left hand: (6a) your left hand does not hold the leash and your arm swings freely at your side or is stationary at your waist, (6b) your left hand holds the leash, palm facing down and placed on your left thigh, (6c) your left and right hands hold the leash jointly, right hand positioned at your waist, left-hand palm facing down placed on your thigh, and (6d) your left hand holds the leash in a manner that allows you to move your hand up and down the leash (see diagram 6).

Diagram 3

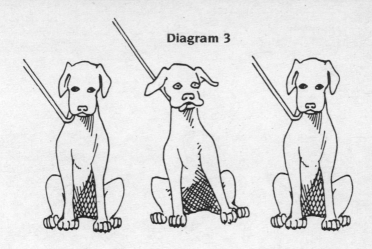

Diagram 4 (a)

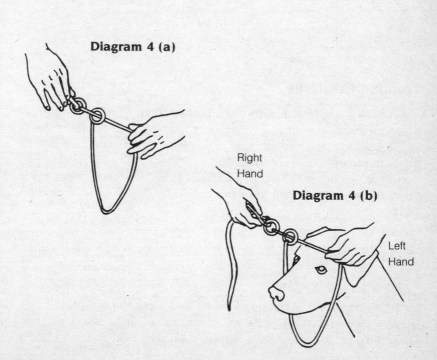

Right
Hand

Diagram 4 (b)

Left
Hand

Diagram 5

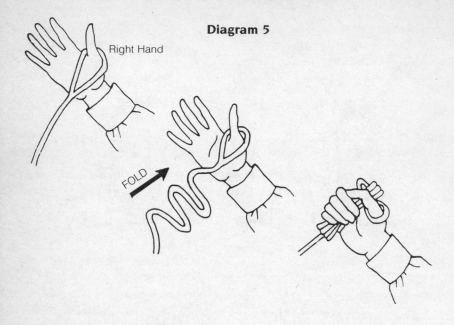

Training Exercises

Five basic obedience skills are common to all training programs. They are teaching your dog to walk on your left side—called *"heeling"*—and to *sit*, lie *down*, *stay* and *come* on command. These are the requirements of a civilized dog.

Before you begin the training exercises, here are some basic rules to follow when you train your dog.

Training Guidelines

Stick to a Schedule

Set aside time for training and follow a regular schedule. Frequency of the training sessions is important. It is better to train frequently for a few minutes during each day than to train once a

Diagram 6

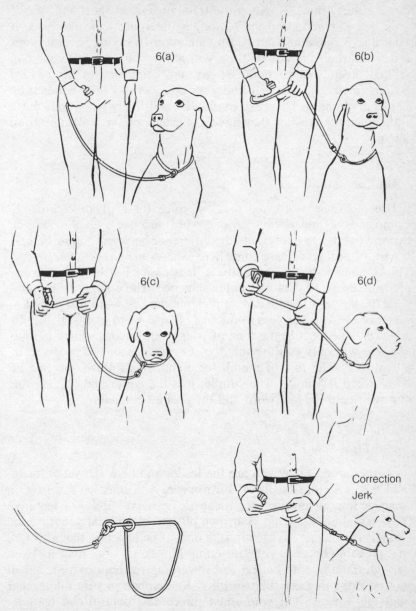

6(a)

6(b)

6(c)

6(d)

Correction
Jerk

day for thirty minutes. Keep the training session short and fun. If your dog is bored, stop the lesson. No learning will take place if your dog is bored and not paying attention. Working several times a day for short periods of time will allow you to teach your dog without losing his attention. If you are using one of the reward training methods, you will find your dog works a little better if he is slightly hungry. Dogs are more alert and lively when they are a little hungry than when they have just eaten or have woken up from a nap.

Be Consistent

Use the same word and tone of voice for a given command. Commands should always be one word and one syllable. Do not expect your dog to understand the difference between "come here," "here," "will you please come here" or "come on, get over here." The command should be "come." It is easier for the dog to comprehend one word than a complex sentence. The dog needs to know what the key word is; he cannot pick out the key word in a complex sentence. Thus, keep your commands to one word, one syllable. In addition never change the tone of your voice; inconsistency in tone of voice will only confuse the dog. Commands should be given in a firm tone. The rule of thumb for commands follows the rule of KIS—Keep It Simple. The simpler it is the easier and quicker the dog will learn the key word and the desired behavior.

Be Firm

Let your dog know you are the leader and he is the subordinate, and this is serious business. Firm means you must be assertive in your actions; firm does not mean to be harsh. Being a tentative person and not knowing your own objectives will only confuse the dog. Do not make excuses for the dog. If he is acting like a clown, it's probably because you are letting him be one—correct it. Even though training is to be fun and rewarding for both of you, it will not be if the dog acts like an idiot. Remember you are the teacher and the leader. *You* who must direct and control the learning environment.

Be Patient

Do not expect results overnight. Most formal training classes run for eight weeks. If you are having a bad day or you are angry or impatient, do not attempt to train your dog until you have calmed down and are in a better frame of mind. A dog will sense your bad attitude, and all that will do is cause an unpleasant training lesson. The dog does not have a complete understanding of what it is you are trying to teach him anyway, so why make it worse? Do not get upset with yourself or your dog if he is not a brilliant pupil. Every person and dog has his learning curve. *Be patient*. It takes time to train any animal, including a dog. When you start training your dog make sure you are happy with what he has learned before you move on to the next exercise.

Respond Immediately

Praise or correct immediately following your dog's behavior to your command. When he comes to your command, lavishly praise him as soon as he gets there. In the training exercise you will encourage the dog through praise even when he attempts to perform the command and did not do it correctly. It is the scheduling and frequency of the praise that will get the end result. Corrections in the program are simple and quick. Depending on the training method you will either give a quick jerk on the leash or physically place the dog in the correct position. Corrections are *not punishment— never hit or strike a dog for performing the exercise incorrectly*. Think of it this way: When you were in school learning to recite the multiplication table and you gave the wrong answer, the teacher did not raise her voice, hit you or berate you. She simply worked the problem through for you until you understood where you erred so that the next time she called on you, you were able to give the correct response. Dog training is no different. A well-trained dog should respond because he wants to please his master, not because he is afraid of you: Fear will only make the dog nervous.

Maintain a Positive Attitude

Always end a training session on a good note. Both of you should feel pleased and happy about the training session. It is absolutely vital to do this if you are to succeed in training your dog. You and your dog need to have a positive attitude toward training, and it is all up to you.

Establishing Eye Contact

Get your dog's attention by saying his name or "WATCH ME" in a happy tone of voice and establish eye contact.

One method of reinforcing eye contact is to lead the dog on a leash as follows: (1) You and your dog should be facing the same direction with the dog next to you on your left side. Hold the leash in your right hand. (2) Look down at the dog and walk forward at

a brisk pace while maintaining him at your side, and say the dog's name or "WATCH ME." (Some instructors have also found it useful to slap their leg with their free hand or use food enticement to get their dog's attention.) (3) After several steps, stop, regain eye contact and say the dog's name or "WATCH ME." (4) Then walk forward again saying the dog's name or "WATCH ME."

Coaching Tips

When starting a new training exercise, reward your dog upon attempting to complete the exercise. The scheduling of the reward changes as your dog learns to associate the task with the reward. When your dog has shown you that he understands the command and task, you should reward him only when he completes the task correctly. This means you would reward your dog only every second or third time he performs the task.

Training Exercises	Obedience Skill
1	Sit
2	Stand
3	Heel
4	Stay
5	Come
6	Down

Exercise 1—Sit

Objective:

To teach your dog to sit on command by either (1) physically placing your dog into position, (2) using food enticement to position the dog, or (3) using the collar and leash to place your dog into position.

Directions:

A. Physical Placement

1. You and your dog should be facing the same direction, with your dog standing at your left side.
2. Kneel, place your right hand on your dog's chest in front of and in between his forelegs. Place your left hand on your dog's back between his shoulders and use it to gently stroke the dog's back toward his tail.
3. Tuck his rear end into position—keeping equal pressure on both left and right hands. Your right hand keeps the dog from moving forward as your left hand tucks his rear end underneath him. As you begin to apply pressure, give the command ''sit.''

4. Hold your dog in position while kneeling next to him for a count of three to five seconds, praising the dog while he is sitting.

B. Food Enticement, Reward

1. Have your dog stand in front of you for this exercise.

2. Hold the enticement object (food reward) just above your dog's nose and slowly move it back toward his tail (stopping about midway over your dog's back). The object is to have your dog raise his head and eyes, following the motion of your hand with the food. As your dog moves his head up and back, he should sit. Hold the object securely; do not let the dog snatch the object from your hand.

3. Give the command ''sit'' just before his rear end begins to go down.

4. Reward your dog with the food upon completion of the sit. Do not give the reward unless your dog takes the food gently.

C. Collar and Leash

1. You and your dog should be facing the same direction, with your dog standing at your left side.

2. Hold the leash in your right hand and raise it by pulling upward gently. The leash should be taut. Simultaneously, place your left hand on your dog's rump and gently push him down into the sit position. If your dog resists your hand on his rump, move your hand further down his rump and apply pressure downward and forward to tuck his rear end underneath him.

3. Give the command ''sit'' as the dog begins to go into the sit position.

4. Hold the dog in position for a count of three to five seconds, and praise the dog.

REPEAT EXERCISE 5 TIMES
COMMAND WORD: SIT

Exercise 2—Stand

Objective:

To teach your dog to stand on command by either (1) physically placing your dog into position, (2) using food enticement to position the dog, or (3) using the collar and leash to place your dog in position.

Directions:

A. Physical Placement

1. Start with the dog in the sit position. Kneel on his right side, move your right hand up and under the dog's muzzle, placing your thumb inside the dog's collar and cradle his muzzle under your palm. Place your left hand under the dog's belly in front of his rear legs.

2. Simultaneously, gently pull your dog forward with your right hand, while applying upward pressure with the left hand under the dog's belly, giving the command "stand." When you gently pull your dog forward with the right hand, be sure not to pull him too far forward out of position.

3. Hold your dog in position for a count of three to five seconds, praising the dog while he remains in the stand position.

B. Food Enticement, Reward

1. While your dog is sitting, hold the object (food reward) in front of and slightly above your dog's nose.

2. Move the object slowly forward and away from the dog's nose and give the command "stand" as the dog begins to lean forward to take the food and get up.

3. Reward your dog with the food upon completion of the stand exercise. Give the reward only when the dog will take it gently.

C. Collar and Leash

1. While your dog is in the sit position on your left side, your right hand pulls the leash upward and directly out in front of the dog. Slide your left hand under your dog's belly while applying upward pressure.

2. Give the command "stand" as your dog begins to move into the stand position.

3. Hold your dog in position for a count of three to five seconds. and praise the dog.

REPEAT EXERCISE 5 TIMES
COMMAND WORD: STAND

Exercise 3—Walking your Dog, Heel

Objective:

To heel your dog, with the dog changing pace as necessary to keep his head approximately even with your left knee by using collar and leash with and without food enticement or reward.

Directions:

A. Collar and Leash

1. You and your dog should be facing the same direction, with your dog either sitting or standing at your left side.

2. Hold the loop of the leash in your right hand, folded to take up some of the slack. Your dog is always on your left side and the loop of the leash is always held in your right hand regardless of whether you are right- or left-handed.

3. Hold the leash in your left hand so your hand will be able to slide up and down the leash.

4. Check the position of the rings of your dog's collar. The leash's snap should be hanging down toward the ground. The slack in the leash from where it is attached to your dog's collar up to your left hand should look like a big U.

5. Place the dog in position.

6. Say the dog's name or "watch me," pause.

7. Then say your dog's name, give your dog the command "heel" and a quick little jerk forward on the leash (in the direction you are heading), and start walking, leading with your left leg. Praise the dog, using his name to encourage him to remain in the heel position. For example: "Mikie, (pause for a few seconds to make sure you have your dog's attention, then give the command) Mikie, Heel! Good boy, Mikie, that's a good dog."

8. Stop after about ten feet and place your dog in the sit position.

9. Repeat the exercise five times.

10. Once your dog has learned "heel" change your walking speed and repeat the exercise five times.

11. Once your dog has learned "down" (exercise 6), repeat the exercise five times, alternating your walking speed and having the dog lie down instead of sit.

B. Food Enticement, Reward

1. Place your dog in the sit position on your left side.

2. Hold the enticement object (food reward) in your left hand, at about your dog's nose level and slightly ahead of him.

3. Start walking forward at a brisk pace. Give the command "heel." Stop and sit your dog and reward him in the sit position.

4. Repeat the exercise, rewarding the dog only when he performed the task better than previously.

5. Once your dog has learned "heel," change your walking speed and repeat the exercise five times.

6. Once your dog has learned "down" (exercise 6), repeat the exercise five times, alternating your walking speed and having the dog lie down instead of sit.

COMMAND WORD: HEEL

Note: In competition, your dog must sit automatically without a verbal command.

Corrections for Heeling Errors

1. Forging—your dog is pulling you forward or rushing ahead of you. Give a quick jerk straight back on the leash and praise your dog as he returns to the heeling position.
2. Lagging—your dog is behind you and not keeping up with your speed. Give a quick jerk forward on the leash and exuberant praise as your dog comes forward into the correct heeling position.

Exercise 4—Stay

Objective:

To teach your dog to remain in the stay position and not move from the position until told to do so by either (1) physically placing your dog into position using a collar and leash, or (2) using food enticement or reward.

Directions:

A. Collar and Leash

1. You and your dog should be facing the same direction, with your dog standing on your left side.

2. Place your dog in the sit position, using the correct command-activity-praise sequence.

3. Rotate your dog's collar so that both rings are directly behind and midway between your dog's ears.

4. Fold the leash in your right hand so there is no slack. The leash should be taut.

5. Bring your left hand out and around in front of your dog's face in one sweeping movement, stopping abruptly in front of his nose. The palm of your hand should be facing the nose. This movement is called the stay hand signal.

6. Maintain tension on the leash while simultaneously giving the stay hand signal and the command "stay."

7. Move in front of your dog and turn facing him. Have your dog hold the position for three to five seconds.

8. Pivot back to your original position next to your dog and release him from the stay position by giving the command "okay." Release the tension on the leash and praise your dog.

9. Repeat the exercise five times.

10. Once your dog has learned ''down'' (exercise 6), repeat the exercise five times, placing your dog in the down position.

Practice

1. Repeat the exercise, gradually increasing the count to ten, fifteen, and twenty-five seconds. The goal is to have your dog sit and stay for one minute.

2. Once your dog has held the sit-stay position for a count of twenty-five seconds, gradually increase the distance you are standing in front of the dog. You should now be working with a slack leash. The goal is to reach the end of the leash, six feet.

3. Repeat the exercise, with your dog in the down position. Correct your dog if he moves out of position.

Correction for Staying Errors

1. If your dog should try to break the stay position, take one step toward the dog while simultaneously giving a quick little jerk on the leash upward and back and give the command ''stay.'' For correcting a down-stay, jerk the leash down and back and give the command ''stay.''

2. Repeat the sequence until your dog will hold the sit or down-stay position for five to ten seconds.

3. As an alternative approach for a down-stay problem, give the stay command, using both verbal and hand signals, then give the dog one foot of slack and step on the leash to prevent your dog from getting up. As your dog tries to get up the leash and collar will become taut. You can also place your left hand on the dog's back between the shoulders and apply gentle downward pressure to get him back into the down position, and try again. Once your dog will hold the position for five to ten seconds, repeat the exercise without stepping on the leash, then work into moving in front of your dog.

 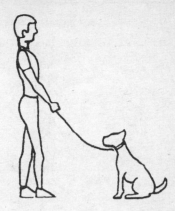

Returning to the Original Position Once You Are Working with a Slack Leash

1. You are facing your dog, and have worked up to a slack leash with the dog remaining in position for at least fifteen seconds.

2. Hold the leash in your right hand. Walk toward the dog, go behind him and stop when you have reached your original starting position. Keep your dog on your left side when you are walking back and around him.

B. Food Enticement, Reward—Sit, Stay

1. Place your dog in the sit position.

2. Move out and pivot in front of your dog so you are facing him.

3. While your dog is in the sit position and your left hand is in front of the dog's nose, take a few steps backward giving the "stay" hand signal and verbal command "stay." Stop momentarily and return to the dog. Reward your dog in the sit position. Gradually increase the length of time the dog sits and stays before you give him the reward. Then reward him only when he performs the task better than previously.

4. Repeat the exercise, but this time move back a few feet, stop, return to the dog and reward the dog in the sit position.

5. Repeat the exercise five times. Continue practicing until the dog will stay for a full minute and you are able to be at least six feet away.

C. Food Enticement, Reward—Down-Stay

1. Place your dog in the sit position, then in the down position (see exercise 6). While facing the dog gradually walk back a few feet, giving the "stay" hand signal and verbal command "stay." Stop, then return to the dog and reward him while he is in the down position.

2. As the dog stays, reward him only when he performs better than previously.

3. Repeat the exercise five times. Continue practicing until your dog will stay for a full minute and you are able to be at least six feet away.

Correct a sit or down-stay when the dog decides to follow you and the food. To do so, walk toward the dog and place him in the desired position, give hand signal and verbal "stay" command, then walk back a few steps and repeat the command "stay." Stop momentarily, then walk back to the dog and reward him in the position he was put in, sit or down.

COMMAND WORD: STAY

Exercise 5—Come

Objective:

To teach your dog to come on command. You should be able to recall your dog using the command "come" in a happy tone of voice. Use with or without food enticement, for encouragement to come on command. Praise the dog as he follows you.

Directions:

1. Place the dog in the sit position using the command "sit."
2. Walk backward while facing the dog, 8 to 10 feet, using the command "come," reeling in the leash as the dog approaches.
3. Stop, repeat exercise five times.

4. After your dog has learned the "stay" command and your dog is working on a slack leash and will stay for a minute, use the command "come" instead of returning to your dog.

5. While the dog is staying, move 6 feet from your dog, turn and face your dog, then call your dog: "Mikie, come!" Reel in the leash as your dog comes forward.

6. When your dog is in front of you, give the command "sit."

7. Repeat the exercise 5 times.

8. Repeat the exercise from the Down/Stay position.

Note: In competition, the judge will tell you to return your dog to the heel position—also called a finish.

Exercise 6—Down

Objective:

To get your dog into the down position by either (1) physically placing your dog into position, or (2) using food enticement and reward.

Directions:

A. Physical Placement

1. You and your dog should be facing the same direction, with your dog in the sit position at your left side.

2. Kneel beside your dog. Place your left hand over the dog's shoulders and underneath his chest and gently grasp his left

foreleg. Place your right hand on your dog's right foreleg from underneath the dog's chest. Cup each of your dog's front legs, one in each hand, and slide and push them forward, giving the command word "down."

3. Hold your dog in position for three to five seconds, praising your dog.

4. Allow your dog to get into the sit position, and repeat this exercise five times.

B. Food Enticement, Reward

1. Put your dog in the sit position on your left side, facing you. Hold a small piece of food in your right hand. Hold the object just above and slightly in front of your dog's nose. Slowly move the object down toward the ground and move it forward away from the dog.

2. As the dog begins to lean forward toward the object, give the command "down." Place your left hand on top of your dog's shoulders to prevent him from getting up.

3. Hold your dog into position for three to five seconds and give him his reward, providing that he takes it gently.

4. Allow your dog to get into the sit position, then repeat this exercise five times.

COMMAND WORD: DOWN

Obedience Class

Now that you have been exposed to the basic training exercises, you may want to pursue more advanced obedience training and compete in obedience trials. You will find that additional training skills will be needed, including use of hand signals instead of verbal commands and exercises conducted without a leash requiring your dog to return to the heel position—also known as the finish.

Many people prefer to attend obedience classes taught by qualified dog trainers and offered by many local kennel clubs, obedience clubs, and humane organizations. For information about the Responsible Dog Owners Program contact "RDOP," c/o The Responsible Dog Owners Association, P. O. Box 173, Fountainville, PA 18923.

7

Common Behavioral Problems
in Dogs

THE SECRET OF SOLVING CANINE BEHAVIORAL PROBLEMS LIES IN identifying their causes. While a little common sense will usually help you to discover the reason behind inappropriate behavior, there are situations that call for the deductive powers of a Sherlock Holmes.

This chapter contains guidelines for interpreting your dog's misbehavior. However, dogs have a limited number of ways to act out, and each dog uses these behaviors a little differently. Because of this, you shouldn't be reluctant to seek professional help if your dog's behavior gets out of hand. There are some situations in which the assistance of an objective, trained professional is the only solution.

Stress

Dogs, like people, may experience stress. Stress can lead to behavioral problems by affecting a dog's ability to react quickly and appropriately. A stressed out dog is an anxious and fearful dog. Signs of stress can include sudden weight gain or loss, weakness, depression, appetite changes and changes in elimination patterns, and unusual behavior. These signs also can indicate physical problems, so it's worth a visit to the veterinarian if they continue for any length of time.

A sudden change in the dog's health or behavior often can be linked to a sudden change in the dog's environment, a deviation from his regular schedule. However, it is important to point out that most dogs do not become unduly stressed by the little upsets and changes that happen in most households.

By working to familiarize your dog with new situations and easing him into schedule changes, you can help your dog to avoid undue stress. For example, if the dog is to be kennelled for the first time, you can take him for a "preview" of the kennel. This will give you an idea of how he will react to being there. Young puppies and small dogs can be carried in your arms before being allowed to explore a new place. This gives them a chance to get used to new sights, sounds and smells while being reassured by your proximity. In general, the best approach is to think ahead and introduce your dog to new things gradually.

Separation Anxiety

Our first dog Drifter, being a stray, was not comfortable when I had to leave her. One time, I ran into the grocery store leaving Drifter behind in our truck because I was in a hurry. She was so upset she soon jumped out of the half-opened window of the truck and ran through the supermarket in search of me.

JOAN EMBERY

~

Separation anxiety, the emotional stress from being left alone, is a very common problem. Sometimes it results in howling, crying and barking. Other times it results in destructive behavior such as chewing the walls, the sofa and everything else in reach.

Dogs are highly social animals and form social attachments which arc essential to their health. Just as children form bonds with their parents, dogs bond with their human family members. A child on the first day of school sometimes engages in increased activity and vocalization about his distress over being separated. Dogs also engage in increased activity and vocalize their distress over being separated from their "parents."

The anxious dog will whine, howl, bark, chew, scratch and may dig at entrance and exits. He does all this to be united with the separated family member. A house trained dog may urinate and defecate throughout the house when he is suffering from separation anxiety. This has nothing to do with the effectiveness of training or dominance/submission. Many animals, including humans, regress to an earlier stage of development in stressful situations.

Anxiety may even occur when the dog and master are separated by a door. If the dog is outside or just in another room with a closed door, he may still show anxiety symptoms. Anxiety can occur with all dogs, purebred or mixed breed. It may occur with the dog that previously has never been left alone or when he is left alone only on rare occasions. A dog may show anxiety following a long interval of separation, such as the family vacation, or after a briefer but traumatic separation, such as the dog getting lost or impounded.

It's up to you to teach your dog that what he initially perceived as being a stressful situation really isn't. You will need to gradually teach him to tolerate being left alone.

One way to do this is to practice sit/stay or down/stay exercises. The goal of this is to have the dog not follow when you walk away. You should be able to move out of the dog's sight and have him remain in the stay position. Practice at different times during the day and alternate your own behavior when he is in the stay position. Go into the kitchen on one exercise and to the living room on the next. And remember that frequent, short training sessions are better than one long one.

Once your dog can handle you leaving his sight by going into another room, step outside. Increase the time you stay outside while allowing the dog to observe you. Then work toward closing the door and coming right back in. Then gradually work toward staying outside a little longer each time. Each time you return to the dog, praise him and give him a treat.

Repeat each exercise enough times to ensure that the dog is not anxious. You can then start to gradually lengthen your absences. Increase the length of the absence first by seconds, then by minutes. Increase your absence duration randomly. The dog should not anticipate your return. By the time he can tolerate 30 minutes alone, most dogs will quickly jump to an hour, then several hours, then longer.

Retraining your dog to be less anxious can be a very long and slow process. Do not move to the next step until you see an improvement in the dog's behavior.

Your dog may get anxious before you leave, as if he is reading your mind that you're going. Actually, he is reacting to a "leaving" cue that you give him. He may have learned to associate your keys, coat, shoes or suitcases with separation. If this is the problem, try doing all of the things your normally do before you leave the house. But this time, don't leave. You must desensitize your dog's association with the cue. Change your behavior and your dog will change his!

Fear

Common fears in dogs are associated with loud sounds, such as thunder, firecrackers, backfires, gunshots, motorcycles, trucks, etc.; to sudden, startling movements of unfamiliar objects; and to unfamiliar people or other animals. Some dogs seem to be shy and overly sensitive from puppyhood and other dogs only develop a fear after a traumatic experience later in life.

Punishing a dog for fearful behavior is likely to be counterproductive. Likewise, forcing a dog to face a very fearful stimulus only makes the problem worse. If the fear is at a high level, you will have to gradually desensitize it. That means identifying the fear stimulus accurately, figuring out some way to present it to the dog at a very low stimulus level, and then very gradually increasing the stimulus level up to maximum without inducing fear.

For example, if the sound of a thunderstorm record or tape will "fake out" the dog, then it is relatively easy to start playing it softly several times a day, and over a few weeks to a month at high level without the dog being afraid. Likewise, a cooperative stranger that the dog fears could visit for very short periods, toss the dog a special food treat and then leave. After several such sessions, it might be possible to get a little closer to the dog or speak to it softly. "Slow but steady" is the key to getting the dog used to things he fears.

Submissive/Excited Urination

Submissive urination is typically seen in young puppies when they are approached by a dominant individual or dog, or upon greeting a returning owner or canine friend. It's usually accompanied by other body postures such as a lowered head and neck, the tail down and wagging and the ears down and held flat against the head.

Never punish or frighten a dog who is engaged in submissive urination. It could have detrimental effects on his emotions. In most cases, a puppy will become more confident and will stop the submissive urination as he grows up. He may, however, retain the other submissive body postures. There is nothing wrong with them, but if you find them disturbing, you can work to gradually build the dog's confidence with training, reassurance and praise. Otherwise, leave the dog alone.

The difference between an excited dog and a submissive dog is seen in the body posture. A dog that urinates out of excitement will not lower his head and neck. Instead, he will dribble as he is walking or running, or will quickly squat in a normal urination posture as he is on his way to greet you. This is not behavior you should punish or correct. When the puppy is older and has more control over his bladder, this urination behavior will usually stop.

Urine Marking in the House

Urine marking involves depositing small puddles of urine at numerous locations—not a problem if the dog is restricted to outdoors, but a definite problem in the house. Marking is usually associated with an unneutered male who has already passed puberty. Because urine marking is so influenced by male hormones, neutering is the most effective solution.

If your dog marks only specific pieces of furniture, try rearranging the room to put your dog's food or bed near that spot. Dogs tend not to urinate or defecate in eating and sleeping areas. Clean the marked areas thoroughly with a non-ammonia cleaner or an odor neutralizer/enzyme product. Don't use ammonia—it smells like urine and will encourage future incidents.

You might change the dog's marking behavior by giving an immediate correction. The correction must occur within the first second of the behavior (thus difficult to do if your urine marker is sneaky), and must not be so severe that the dog develops a fear (of you!).

The correction is meant to disturb the behavior. Never hit the dog, as physical punishment is ineffective. Also, if the dog has dominant or aggressive tendencies, he may respond to hitting with hostility. It is better to disrupt the behavior by squirting water at him, or shouting a loud "HEY" command, or "NO."

If the dog marks in very specific situations, such as when the doorbell rings and a visitor enters, you can condition him to exhibit an alternative behavior, such as sitting or fetching a toy, to replace the marking behavior.

Solving Behavior Problems

The key to solving canine behavior problems is to try to understand how dogs perceive things. Put yourself in your dog's position. Remember that you are the leader. Your dog looks to you for guidance, leadership, safety and security. Play the leader's role, and help him overcome stressful situations.

When dealing with stress, identify, examine and evaluate stressful situations. Determine the causes of your dog's anxious behaviors and fearful responses. Then work to alleviate your dog's stress either by changing the stress stimulus, or by changing—desensitizing—your dog.

Most important, use common sense and be considerate with your dog. Pay attention to your dog's physical and emotional needs, his daily routines and what to him are crisis situations. Spend time with him and show him you care. Dogs are social creatures and need your companionship and love to reassure them. They will be looking for an opportunity to return that love and companionship—and may surprise you when you need a little reassurance yourself.

8

Grooming

Traveler, our frisky yellow Labrador Retriever, loves the water. In fact, keeping her out of it—be it pond, pool or bath—is much harder than getting her into it. Our biggest problem is that she loves to play and roll around in the mud, preferably just after she's had a bath.

JOAN EMBERY

~

ALL DOGS NEED REGULAR GROOMING. REGULAR GROOMING removes dead hair, dander and dirt. It stimulates the blood supply to the skin and results in a healthier and shinier coat.

Start grooming your puppy as soon as he is comfortable with his new surroundings. You may find that at first the puppy will not like it, but then he will settle down and enjoy it. The pup will also enjoy being fondled and talked to when you groom him. Buy the proper grooming equipment; don't use one of your old brushes. Either ask the breeder from whom you got the dog what type of grooming equipment you'll need or ask a local groomer. The type of grooming equipment you'll need will depend on the type of hair coat your dog has. Most typically, currycombs are used on short-haired dogs (for example, Beagles, Labrador Retrievers, Boxers). A currycomb is oval shaped, fits in the palm of your hand, and usually has either rubber or metal saw shaped (serrated) teeth. Longer toothed combs and pin brushes are recommended for long-haired dogs (for example, Afghans, Poodles, Golden Retrievers).

Grooming also includes trimming your dog's nails. Trimming nails, if you've never done it before, can be quite tricky. If you can hear your dog's nails go tick, tick, tick across a hardwood or tile floor, they are too long. Ask your veterinarian to show you how to trim your dog's nails. If you cut the nail too far back, it will bleed, and continue to bleed, and you'll be convinced it will never stop bleeding. There are nail clippers especially designed for dogs as well as a product known as "Quick Stop," a powder that you can apply to stop the toenail from bleeding.

Grooming is also a good time to teach your puppy to be handled. Getting your puppy accustomed to being handled is a step-by-step process. It is a good time to teach him restraint so in the future he will stand or sit quietly for grooming, checkups or examinations by the veterinarian. You can't groom your puppy or examine him if he is running around.

Restraint Exercises

Kneel on the floor and have your puppy sit in the space between your legs. You and he are facing the same direction. Place one of your hands in front of his chest to prevent him from running off, and with your free hand, begin to stroke him and praise him. Hold him there a few seconds. If your puppy is squirming and does not want to sit still, give him a firm "no" and go on with the exercise. If the firm no does not make him stop squirming for a few seconds, then give the command "no" and gently give him a shake, holding on to the scruff of his neck. If your puppy is of the rowdy type, it may take both your hands to hold him still. Don't grab his legs to make him hold still, just his chest. Talk to him, and once he settles down, praise him and pet him. This exercise should continue until he is willing to sit quietly for a minute without being restrained. This may take a couple of weeks. You should practice this a couple of times a day for a few seconds, gradually increasing the time he is to sit still. This holds true for all the exercises. Little by little increase the time the pup is to be still. And little by little increase those areas you want to handle and hold.

Once your puppy is sitting between your knees for a minute without moving, take your hands and run them down his legs, touch his feet and run your hand back up his leg. Praise him and pet him as usual. Your goal is being able to pick his feet up and hold them in your hands. Once you can hold his feet in your hand, gently hold on to each toe. This is to prepare him for having his nails clipped. Most dogs hate their feet being touched and held. If you start now he'll accept it in the future. Once you have mastered him sitting still and handling his front legs, it is time to work on the back legs.

With your puppy in the same position, run your hands down his hind leg, rub his belly a little and touch his hind feet. You won't be able to pick up his hind feet while he is sitting, so don't try. Once you have accomplished this exercise, move on to the next. With the dog lying on his side, start the process all over again.

After he can lie on his side and be still, begin sliding him gently from side to side. If he becomes used to being pushed from side to side, he will be more willing to accept being pushed off your favorite chair when he is older. Also when he is lying still, check his ears, stroke them and gently lift them up as though you were checking for ticks. Run your hands over his muzzle and his lips. Pick up his lip and look at his teeth. The key to successfully having your dog lie or sit still to be examined is time and patience. This is a long process. Don't rush the puppy and don't expect the puppy to be perfect; after all, he is only a playful puppy. When all is said and done, you and your puppy will find this a quiet and relaxing exercise.

Training a dog to respond properly to restraint while he is a puppy is essential because a puppy is easier to handle than an adult dog. The previous restraint exercises will result in a dog who behaves properly when handled by you or other people.

9

Canine Nutrition

DOGS ARE BASICALLY CARNIVORES—MEAT EATERS. THEY AREN'T limited to meat, though. Dogs can use a wide variety of food stuffs efficiently to meet their nutritional requirements.

Within limits dogs regulate their food intake to meet their energy requirements. They'll eat a sufficient quantity of food based on the diet's formulation and the amount of energy available for them to digest. However, given free access to a highly digestible, high nutrient density food, many dogs overeat, resulting in obesity, the most common nutritional disease of adult dogs today.

What a Dog Needs

A dog needs the same basic building blocks of nutrition as any other animal: proteins, carbohydrates, fats, vitamins and minerals.

Carbohydrates, fat and protein supply the dog with energy. When carbohydrates or fat are used for energy, protein is freed up for building and maintaining the body.

Proteins can come from both plants and animals. In plants, the protein is concentrated in the actively growing leaves and in seeds such as corn kernels, wheat grains and soybeans. In animals, proteins are more widely distributed. They are the primary constituents of most body tissues. Proteins in most commercial pet foods come primarily from organs and muscles, since hair, hooves and skin are specifically prohibited from use. Some ligament and bone are also used. Protein supplies the body with the building materials for the synthesis of enzymes and muscle tissues.

Proteins are made up of a string of subunits called amino acids. Amino acids are the building blocks of proteins. There are twenty common amino acids. Ten are called essential amino acids because the dog's body cannot manufacture them in sufficient quantities. These essential amino acids must be provided in the diet in order for the dog to thrive. The amino-acid content of individual proteins vary. The ability of a protein to meet the dog's amino-acid requirement depends on the source and quality of the protein supplied in the diet. It must be palatable (taste good), digestible (absorbed by the body) and metabolizable (utilizable).

Good sources of amino acids include muscle meats and nontendinous organs (i.e., liver, lungs, kidneys, etc.), eggs, dairy products and soybeans. Most dog foods are formulated with a selected combination of the above sources to achieve the best mixture of amino acids.

Some proteins will provide more of one amino acid than another. The source of the protein will have an impact on the amino acid content. For example, corn is deficient in the amino acid lysine. A source of lysine must be added to corn-based foods to meet the requirement. Beef and soybean meal, for example, are very high in lysine. Pet food manufacturers use a variety of protein sources in formulating their foods so proper ratios and levels of all amino acids are present and available to the dog.

Each dog, depending on his stage of growth, age and activity level, will require a different level of protein in his diet. For example, an older, inactive dog may need as little as 16 percent crude protein in the diet, while a female nursing puppies may need as much as 25 percent crude protein, provided good-quality protein sources are used in the formulation. Both of these protein requirements are easily met by a number of commercially available dog foods. The guaranteed analysis on the bag tells you the minimum amount of crude protein you'll find in the food. The guaranteed analysis does not tell you anything about the level of essential amino acids, however, nor their availability. For this you must know your manufacturer.

Carbohydrates are abundant in plants and occur in a variety of forms. They are combinations of sugars, ranging from the simple sugars to complex starches. Carbohydrates are an economical source of energy for man and dogs. Dogs utilize carbohydrates with an efficiency equal to that of humans. An animal who eats carbohydrates frees proteins essential for building the body instead of being used as an energy source. Carbohydrates can supply up to 60 percent of the dietary calories required. The primary role of carbohydrates is to provide the dog with energy. That's why they're one of the major sources of energy in dog foods.

There are a variety of carbohydrate sources, some more digestible than others. The kernels from corn and wheat are more digestible and provide a better source of carbohydrates than, for example, the indigestible cellulose of the stems and stalks of the same plants. Digestible carbohydrates in dog food are cooked, as the cooking process improves digestibility as well as palatability.

Lactose, a carbohydrate and a sugar found only in milk, is poorly digested by older dogs. Cow's milk has a higher lactose content than dog's milk does, and should not be substituted for it as a puppy formula. Cow's milk will ferment in the puppy's lower digestive tract and cause diarrhea. Dog-milk substitutes specifically formulated for orphaned puppies are commercially available.

Fats and oils in dog foods are the principle source of the essential fatty acid linoleic acid, as well as direct sources of linolenic acid, which is believed by many to promote healthy skin and to help the dog's coat to look bright and shiny. Fats are also carriers of the essential fat-soluble vitamins and vital for proper absorption of these vitamins from the food. Fats function as a concentrated source of energy, since when metabolized, they liberate twice as much energy as carbohydrates. To meet their energy needs, dogs need smaller quantities of properly balanced foods high in fat than of such foods with less fat.

Dogs can tolerate rations that are up to 50 percent fat. This, however, is not economically feasible or practical. The higher the fat content, the less food the dog should eat overall. All of the essential nutrients in these formulas must then be readjusted to maintain a proper balance of nutrients to calories.

During the manufacture of dry dog foods fats are stabilized with antioxidants to retard spoilage or rancidity. When fats become rancid, the fat-soluble vitamins A, D, E and K are also destroyed. Foods taste bad when made with rancid fats. So antioxidants are used to keep the fat fresh. Some of the more commonly used are BHA and ethoxyquin. Recently, some manufacturers have started using natural antioxidants such as vitamin E (mixed—tocopherols) and vitamin C (ascorbic acid). While these are not as efficient at preserving the fat, they make people feel better about feeding fewer chemicals—and they can be called "all natural." This, however, is not necessarily of any nutritional advantage.

Dogs need *vitamins*. They are essential for growth and maintenance of good health. A diet lacking in a particular vitamin can produce a variety of nasty symptoms. On the other hand, too much of a particular vitamin, especially fat-soluble vitamins, will produce other adverse effects. Dogs require at least twelve vitamins and twelve minerals, which are supplied in all good commercially prepared dog foods. That's why adding vitamin and mineral supplements to a complete and balanced commercial dog food is unnecessary and potentially harmful. This is particularly true if the manufacturer has proven the nutritional adequacy of the food by feeding it to dogs.

Vitamins are divided into two groups: fat-soluble and water-soluble. The fat-soluble vitamins are A, D, E and K. The water-soluble vitamins include biotin, choline, folic acid, niacin, pantothenic acid, thiamine (B1), riboflavin (B2), pyridoxine (B6) and B12.

Vitamins occur naturally in food and can be purified into a crystalline form. In the manufacture of most dog foods, the processing method destroys some vitamins. These are added in sufficient quantities to the food before processing so the final product has the proper balance and amount of the necessary vitamins at the time it is fed.

Fat-soluble vitamins are, as the name implies, associated with the dietary lipids (fats). They are absorbed from the intestine in fat emulsions called chylomicrons in a manner simular to dietary fat. These vitamins are then stored in the liver and in fatty tissues. Most animals have enough of a reserve to carry them through times of deprivation, although it is best to supply proper amounts in their food daily.

Vitamin A is necessary for the production of visual pigment found in the rod cells of the retina. It is also important for bone growth, reproduction functions and maintenance of epithelial tissue such as skin and the respiratory and digestive tracts.

Young dogs are more susceptible to vitamin A deficiency than adult dogs. Requirements for growth are greater than those for maintenance, since there has not been time to build up reserves.

Some vitamin A deficiency symptoms include stunted growth, loss of weight and appetite, night blindness, reproductive failure, a nervous incoordination (staggering walk) and xerophthalmia, which is an eye disease. Too much vitamin A has been associated with irregular and defective bone growth, and visible signs similar to a deficiency.

Vitamin D is critical to the dog's ability to metabolize calcium and phosphorus. These two minerals are required for bones to develop properly. Without adequate vitamin D, the young will develop rickets and adults will develop osteomalacia—two types of bone deformities.

Vitamin E is an antioxidant. It protects the cell membranes throughout the body from oxidative damage, which changes the nature of the cell. Vitamin E keeps muscles from degenerating and maintains proper reproductive performance.

Vitamin K is essential for normal blood coagulation and clotting. Deficiencies show up in bleeding that doesn't stop.

Water-soluble vitamins are not stored in the body. Daily losses in metabolism occur and excess vitamins are simply excreted in the urine. They must be replaced every day.

The animal is more likely to have a deficiency than a toxicity of water-soluble vitamins. Levels approaching a hundred to a thousand times the minimum requirement are tolerated in the majority of cases.

Thiamine (vitamin B1) promotes a good appetite and normal growth. It is required for basic carbohydrate metabolism and thus energy production. Thiamine deficiency is rare and would be caused by lack of consideration for losses in processing and storage. Thiamine is readily destroyed by oxidation at elevated temperatures. A deficiency will show up as anorexia or cardiovascular disturbances.

Riboflavin (vitamin B2) promotes growth and is involved in several enzyme systems. Thus it is important in carbohydrate, fat and protein metabolism. Puppies need more riboflavin than adult dogs. Deficiency symptoms may include weight loss and dry, flaky skin.

Pyridoxine (vitamin B6) is important to nitrogen metabolism and red blood cell formation. Deficiencies show up as anorexia, poor growth and anemia. In severe cases, convulsions may occur.

Pantothenic acid is required for energy metabolism. It is a component of coenzyme A, and as such participates in the oxidation of carbohydrates, fats and some proteins. Slow growth and erratic appetite are early signs of a deficiency. Severe deficiency results in convulsions and coma.

Niacin is a constituent of two coenzymes that enable cells to release the energy in carbohydrates, proteins and fats. A niacin deficiency in dogs shows up as a darkening of the tongue called black tongue disease. Early signs are the 3 Ds—dermatitis, diarrhea and dementia.

Vitamin B12 is a coenzyme necessary for normal nucleic acid synthesis. It's important for proper folic acid metabolism, so a deficiency in one can lead to a deficiency in the other. Slow or retarded growth is the main symptom of a deficiency. Pernicious anemia, where vitamin B12 is not absorbed properly in the intestine, results in a deficiency, but this is extremely difficult to demonstrate in dogs.

Folic acid is related to B12 metabolism and a variety of other bodily biochemical reactions. Anemia and impaired immune reaponse are associated with folic acid deficiency. Slow growth and poor appetite are also sympltons.

Biotin functions as a coenzyme active in several enzyme systems. Deficiency signs are nonspecific, but dermatitis may be seen.

Choline is involved in proper transmission of nerve impulses. It is also a component of certain fats. Although listed with the vitamins, it does not qualify as a true vitamin and does not participate in any enzyme system.

Vitamin C is not required in the diet of dogs (unlike humans), as adequate amounts are synthesized in the dog's liver. Vitamin C participates in a number of body development functions such as the formation of intracellular substances of the teeth, bone and soft tissue. Scurvy is the classical symptom of vitamin C deficiency in man, with swollen, bleeding gums and loosening of the teeth.

Minerals serve an important function in the diet. They give rigidity and strength to bones and teeth. They're also found in the tissues that make up the muscles, organs and blood cells. They help activate enzyme systems in the body, maintain proper fluid levels, facilitate nerve transmission and other functions.

Minerals are divided into two categories, based on the amount the body needs. The major minerals—calcium, sodium, chlorine, phosphorus, magnesium, and potassium—are needed in larger amounts. Trace minerals—copper, iodine, iron, manganese, selenium and zinc—are needed in very tiny amounts. Chromium, fluorine, molybdenum and silicon, however, need not and should not be added to dog food!

There is a very narrow margin of safety with most of the trace minerals. Too much and they can be toxic. Because of this, extra care must be taken when adding mineral supplements to an already properly mineral-balanced dog food. Mixing a balanced commercial dog food with small amounts of cottage cheese, for example, does not change the relationship between calcium and phosphorus. However, by adding calcium in the form of calcium carbonate or other calcium salts, you do!

For the body to get the most out of minerals in the diet, those minerals must be present in the proper ratio of one to the other as well as in the proper quantity and using the proper sources. For example, calcium and phosphorus will be best utilized when they are provided in a ratio of 1.2 parts calcium to 1 part phosphorus and when normal levels of vitamin D are also supplied. Most commercial dog foods supply vitamins and minerals in their proper balance. It's easy for you to mess up this balance by providing a supplement or a food particularly high in or devoid of one or more essential vitamins or trace minerals.

Some breeders give their dogs extra calcium in the form of calcium carbonate. This can be overdone. Supplemental calcium should not be added to adequate diets, particularly for growing dogs. Here's why: excessive levels of calcium in the food increase the required level in the food for phosphorus, managnese, zinc and copper. High levels of calcium have been shown to increase the need for dietary zinc and manganese; in particular, excess calcium (2.0 percent +) has been demonstrated to result in skeletal deformities when fed during the growing period of members of the large or giant breeds of dogs.

Adding calcium this way may also upset the zinc requirement. Zinc is also found throughout the body, particularly in the skin and hair. Zinc is an essential component of many enzymes and hormones. Adding foods containing calcium can reduce the absorption of zinc, leading to a deficiency. Zinc deficiency shows up as slow growth, inflamed skin around the nose and mouth, stiffness of joints, loss of hair, graying of hair, scaly skin and reproductive problems. Too much zinc, on the other hand, can lead to anemia, as zinc interferes with the use of iron and copper.

As you can see, the mineral balance is quite delicate. That's why it's best, in our opinion, not to add any food or supplements to your dog's already complete and balanced diet.

Dogs also need *water*. A dog's body is composed of approximately 70 percent water, which must be replenished daily. This water intake is partially supplied by its food. However, all dogs should be supplied with fresh drinking water.

Vitamins and Minerals in Commercial Dog Foods

Since vitamins and minerals are such an important part of every dog's diet, and since they work together in such an intricately balanced way, dog food manufacturers are careful to add just the right amounts. They try to ensure that there is an adequate supply of vitamins and minerals in their food, that they are in a form the dog can use and that they are in the proper ratio.

Commercial vitamin-mineral producers provide premixed packages of vitamins and minerals in the proper proportions and forms. The dog food manufacturer usually buys such premixes, which often are custom designed to complement the quantities needed for this particular product. Because the necessary amounts of vitamins and minerals are so small compared with ingredients such as protein and energy sources, these are usually found at the end of the ingredient list. Vitamins and minerals are usually the ones with the longest chemical names.

Added vitamins might include niacin, riboflavin, thiamine mononitrate, D-calcium pantothenate, pyridoxine hydrochloride, vitamin B12, biotin and folic acid (all B vitamins). You may also find vitamin A, vitamin D, and vitamin E. One dog food contains the tongue-twisting menadione dimethylpyrimidinol bisulphite, which is a source of vitamin K, normally produced by bacteria in the dog's intestines.

Minerals in your dog food may include calcium carbonate (calcium), ferrous sulfate (iron), zinc oxide (zinc), copper sulfate (copper) and sodium selenite (selenium). These too appear on the ingredient list.

There *Is* a Difference in Dog Foods

With hundreds of brands of pet food on the market, it's not easy to find the right one for your dog. You need to know about your own dog's special needs, and you need information about nutrition and why one food will satisfy your dog's needs, while another may not.

Let's take a look at the basics: the basic nutrient needs of dogs, the basics of understanding dog food labels, the basics of how a pet food is formulated and the basics of how to choose a food. What are the differences between dog foods, and how can you get the most for your money? Read on and find out.

The most important factor in choosing a dog food is your dog. Even more than people, dogs vary greatly. Some dogs weigh only two pounds, others weigh close to two hundred. Some lead a sedentary life, sleeping the days away. Others are active, running, playing, chasing, hunting. Age makes a difference, too. A young, growing dog needs more power-packed nutrition than an old dog, or even a dog whose growth has come to a halt with adolescence.

Different Types of Dog Food

What's the difference between dog foods? Plenty! Differences include form (dry, semimoist, canned), quality of ingredients, nutritional value and chemicals used.

Let's look at form first. Dry dog food is just that: dry. About 88 percent to 92 percent of the water has been removed, leaving a crunchy food. Semi-moist products such as "burgers" are somewhat soft because they contain 25 percent to 30 percent water. They also contain a whole host of chemical preservatives to fight bacteria and fungi and maintain a long shelf life. Canned dog food usually contains 75 percent to 78 percent water, which is the normal moisture content of fresh meat and is necessary to efficiently heat-sterilize the canned food without destroying all of the heat-sensitive nutrients, like vitamins. Dogs prefer the flavor of canned foods, so many people will mix canned food with dry to improve the dry food's palatability. (This is fine as long as both foods are complete and balanced.)

Dry dog food is usually made from cereal grains (corn, wheat, rice), poultry by-product meal, meat and bone meal, fats, vitamins and minerals. The ingredients are mixed and cooked under high pressure with steam. This mixture is then extruded through a specially shaped nozzle that gives the product its unique shape, something like toothpaste being squeezed from a tube. Next, it is dried and fat and flavors sprayed on for palatability prior to packaging.

Canned dog food, known in the industry as "wet" or "canned meat," comes in several varieties. Some are based on meat and meat by-products, while others contain cereals. They are packaged in hermetically sealed containers (metal or plastic cans, trays or pouches) and heated at high temperatures to achieve commercial sterility.

The heat in the processing of the ingredients destroys undesirable enzymes, but it also destroys some of the B vitamins. Consequently, these are added in extra quantities before the heating.

Be a Better Shopper: Read the Label!

Requirements for labeling dog foods are quite stringent. The label on dog food tells most of the story of what's in the package.

The *name of the product* will give you some clues as to what's inside. A product labeled *"beef* dinner" must contain 25 percent of the named ingredient—beef—by weight, of all the ingredients. Likewise, a "sliced chicken and liver entree" must contain at least 12.5 percent chicken and no more than the same amount of liver for a total of at least 25 percent.

If a product says *"beef* for dogs" it must contain 95 percent of the named ingredient—beef. The other 5 percent of the formula can be used for vitamins, minerals, and other goodies. Also quite common are the "flavored" foods. A beef-flavored product, for example, doesn't have to contain any beef—but it must have the taste of beef. This may be provided by natural or artificial flavors. The rest of the ingredients are likely to be grains and animal by-product meals.

Next look at the *list of ingredients.* You'll find them listed in descending order by weight. While the word *protein* comes from the Greek word meaning "of first rank or importance," this does not necessarily mean that the first ingredient on the list is the primary protein source. It may be the primary source of energy, or in the case of some canned dog food, it can be water.

An area in which labels can be misleading is in the nutritional quality of ingredients. The *nutritional quality of an ingredient* has to do with the amount of nutrients available to the dog from that ingredient.

An important point to remember is that not all of a particular ingredient will be retained and absorbed by the body. Only a certain portion is available for the dog to use. The amount used by the body varies based on the source of the ingredient as well as the body that's using it. Corn may come in different grades, and these may be substituted for each other in the same dog food. The ingredients list doesn't reflect the grade of corn, so a manufacturer could replace an expensive grade with a cheaper one.

Two other factors are the form of the ingredient and the processing method used on the ingredient. For example, iron in the form of iron oxide can't be absorbed by the body, while iron as ferrous sulfate is readily absorbed and used by the body. As for processing, a dog can't digest the hard exterior of a whole grain. Through processing, the interior is exposed and the nutrients become more available.

The *guaranteed analysis* is required information on every pet food and treat label. It tells you the minimum amounts of crude protein and fat and the maximum amount of crude fiber, ash and moisture for the food. These numbers give a rough idea of what you can expect. For example, two foods might each list 21 percent crude protein, but one might be more digestible and thus provide more nutrients to the dog. The nutritional quality of the ingredients makes the difference.

You Get What You Pay For . . . or Do You?

With dog food, you don't always get what you pay for. You can get less than what you pay for or more. It depends on the quality of the ingredients, the formula and the nutritional density of the food.

If you look at cost per feeding, you'll discover an interesting fact: It may cost less to feed a premium or super-premium dog food than an economy dog food. The secret is in the energy content of the food.

For example, in a kennel of seventy active hunting dogs over the last three years, ten different brands of dry dog food ranging from econo brands to super-premiums were tested. We found that it usually doesn't pay to feed a low-quality dog food. The better the nutritional quality of the food, the less it takes to feed your dog. Even at a somewhat higher price per bag, you can save several cents per feeding per dog. Usually, the better quality the food, the better the value.

Of course, there are cases where the high price you pay doesn't translate into a lower cost per feeding. Some of the most expensive dog foods on the market cost more per serving than many lower-cost products with quality ingredients.

One guide to choosing a dog food is to compare the crude protein, fat, crude fiber and moisture content of each brand. Then compare the ingredients and recommended daily serving size. This should give you a basic yardstick for comparison.

Until recently, nobody in the pet food marketplace had set standards for categories of dog food. Standards for each class of dry dog food have been published in the January 1993 issue of *Good Dog!* magazine.

The determination of the category for each food was based on several factors, including the list of ingredients and their quality; guaranteed analysis; digestibility of the food; metabolizable energy (based on how much energy is available for the dog to use); and price per feeding.

Here are some basic rules of thumb, for an adult dry maintenance-type diet. Please note that there is room for plenty of variation within each category.

Economy brands have a low price and usually use lower-quality ingredients. You'll find them at the supermarket and discount houses or feed stores. Economy brands are usually more expensive per feeding than one might expect, as it takes more food to fulfill the dog's nutritional needs.

Another way of looking at economy brands is as a vegetarian diet for dogs. Cereal grains such as corn, wheat and soy head the ingredients list, followed by a meat source. Another big clue is that the food may not have been the subject of an Association of American Feed Control Officials (AAFCO) feeding trial. The "complete and balanced" claim may be substantiated only by chemical analysis. The crude protein value averages 19 percent and the crude fat value averages 8 percent.

Regular brands of dog food are moderately priced, and the nutritional quality of the ingredients are moderate too. The guaranteed analysis will show *at least* 19 percent crude protein and *at least* 8 percent fat. The majority of regular brands will be found at the supermarket. A typical ingredients list on a regular brand will have cereal grains such as corn, wheat, and soybean meal listed prior to any meat source such as meat and bone meal. The majority of these foods will have proof of nutritional adequacy by fulfilling the AAFCO dog feeding protocols.

Premium brands are a step up from regular brands and usually represent a good value. Some premium foods contain soy, others do not. The protein level will be at least 21 percent crude protein and at least 10 percent fat. These foods are quite digestible and contain good-quality protein sources. They are usually the midpriced choices at the supermarkets, and one of the lower-priced options at the pet store. You can't go wrong with most of them, although some are better than others. Premium brands typically list meat sources as the first or second ingredient, followed by cereal grains and soybeans. An ingredients list would start off like this: ground corn, poultry by-product meal, soybean meal. Another example: meat & bone meal, brewer's rice, ground yellow corn.

Super-premium foods have a minimum of 25 percent crude protein and a minimum of 15 percent fat. A typical ingredients list will start with: chicken, chicken or poultry by-products, corn and wheat. Super-premiums contain high quality sources of protein and energy. While the price on the bag may be higher, you'll feed less per meal, so your cost per meal may actually be lower than with an economy or regular brand or some premium foods.

What separates super-premiums and performance foods from all the rest is their high crude protein and fat content, along with the absence of soybeans. Manufacturers of high-protein dog foods have to meet their stated guaranteed analysis for crude protein. They have a choice. They can either use high-quality meat sources and gluten meals or use a lesser-quality meat source and add soybean meal to boost the protein content. Super-premium dog foods use high-quality meat ingredients as their source of protein and do not contain soy. This does not, however, necessarily translate into a superior protein food.

Beware of premium dog foods masquerading as super-premiums. Some foods are priced high enough to be super-premiums, yet the ingredients tell the true story. To determine the best value, compare ingredients and cost per feeding of several brands.

The performance foods are designed for dogs who are performing extra duty, such as sled dogs, hunting dogs and otherwise high-spirited dogs. Performance foods contain no soy, and have a very high protein and fat content. The ingredients will be similar to the super-premium, but the performance foods will have higher levels of protein and fat: a minimum of 30 percent crude protein, 20 percent crude fat.

Shopping for dog food can be a fun experience. Learning about it will certainly keep you off the streets. Read labels, call manufacturers for their literature and give some products a try for a month or two. The bottom line is that the right dog food is the one that keeps your dog healthy and happy at a reasonable cost per feeding.

Reading Labels

Today, dog foods are evaluated for nutritional adequacy by three methods: actual feeding trials, defined reproducible chemical procedures and/or nutritional calculations. The guaranteed analysis gives us but a very limited foundation for evaluating the dog food. What do the terms on the dog food package mean?

Commercially prepared dog foods are required by state laws to be labeled. The laws are coordinated between all of the states by the Association of American Feed Control Officials. Although state laws vary somewhat, most of them require that the labels state the minimum crude protein and the minimum fat content. The label must also show a maximum of crude fiber and moisture content. Many manufacturers include the maximum amount of ash content on the labels of their products, as well.

What do these terms mean? These figures are your assurance that the food contains the minimum stated amount of the higher-cost nutrients—protein and fat. It also ensures that there aren't more of the lower-cost, less nutritionally valuable items in the diet—crude fiber and water.

Crude protein is the first item in the guaranteed analysis. Protein, on the average, contains 16 percent nitrogen. Scientists use this fact as a guide for determining the protein level of the food. If they know the nitrogen content, they can estimate the protein level.

To determine the nitrogen content of a food, a process is used called the Kjeldahl determination. In this process, a sample of the food is destroyed with sulfuric acid. The nitrogen that is liberated is converted into an ammonia compound, then measured. An alternative method (Dumas) involves combusting the food and measuring the nitrogen gases that evolve. From this, the nitrogen content and ultimately the protein content are calculated.

This process of determining the protein content is not very accurate. Now you know why it is called crude protein! Since this method determines only the nitrogen content and other compounds in the food contain nitrogen, it gives only a crude estimate of the protein content.

Crude fat is material that is extracted from moisture-free food by using ether. It consists largely of fats and oils. Small amounts of waxes, resins and coloring matter may also be contained in it. In

Putting on a Collar

In this series, Nan Weitzman demonstrates the correct method of putting on a collar *(see page 65)*.

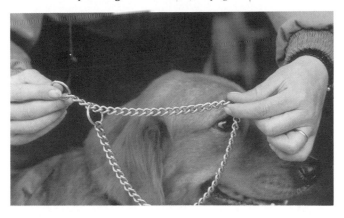

Walking on a Leash

A dog pulling and running is not only wrong, it is also dangerous to the dog's safety—and yours, too!

Here Joan Embery sets the pace and the dog looks up and pays attention. Note how the leash is held in the right hand while the dog walks on the left side.

One Sit Command Method

Joan demonstrates the "food reward method" to teach a dog to sit
(see page 73).

One Down Command Method

Joan demonstrates the "physical displacement" technique to teach a dog to lie down on command *(see page 86)*.

Puppies Playing

Puppies can easily entertain themselves with the simplest household item. Here, two golden retriever puppies play with a towel.

Grooming

Regular grooming is important to a dog's overall health.

Nails should be clipped regularly *(see page 96).*

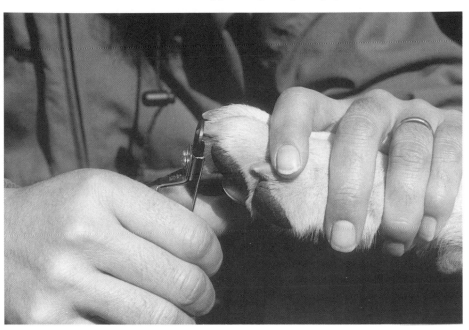

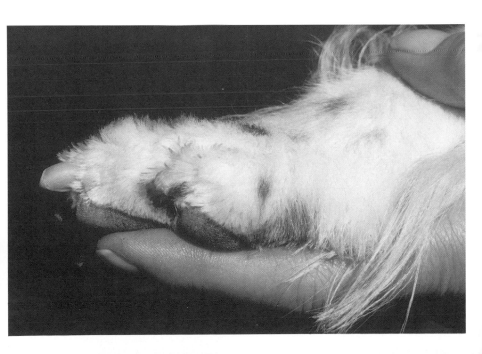

Giving a Dog a Pill

(See page 124).

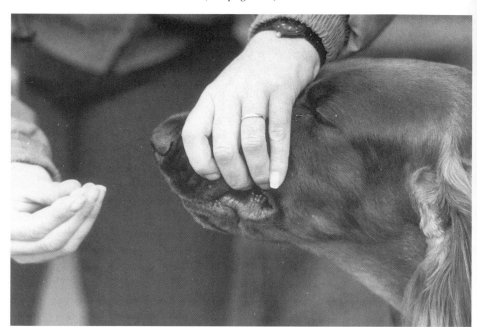

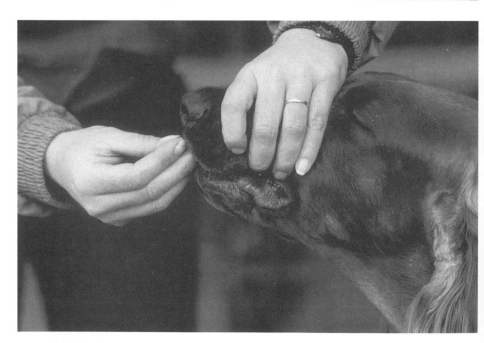

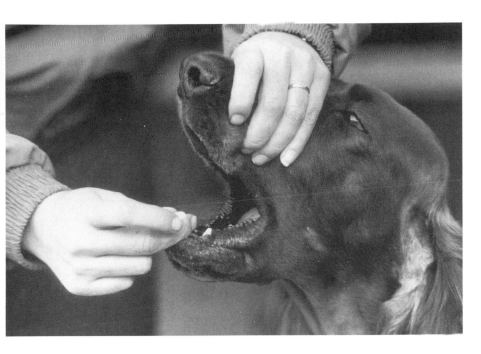

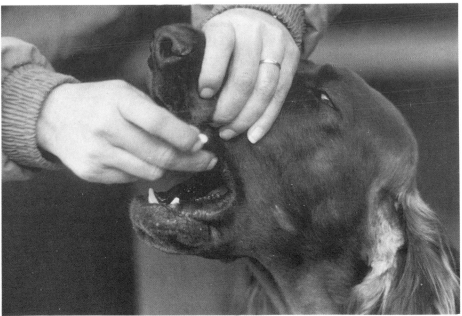

Traveling

For safety, the dog should be in a crate. Be sure to bring along a toy, blanket, water, and bowl.

Dog seat belts are an effective way to safely restrain a dog when traveling.

Pet Etiquette

Curbing your dog is an important part of being a responsible dog owner.

Jumping Up

Jumping up can be a problem because many people are afraid of dogs
(see page 32).

Barking

A dog that barks or howls for hours is a neighborhood nuisance.

Nan Weitzman and Joan Embery with friends.

the analysis of extruded foods, samples must be subject to hydrolysis (cooked in acid) prior to extraction in order to liberate fat bound during extrusion.

The *ash portion* represents the inorganic constituents of the dog food, namely minerals, of which calcium and phosphorus are the major constituents. Samples of the dog food are ignited at temperatures in excess of 600 degrees C. (1112°F.). The residue left after the burning process is called ash. A statement of ash content is not required, although it would be of great value. Without it you cannot calculate the NFE (carbohydrate) content.

The *crude fiber* content of the dog food is some indication of the digestibility and bulk of the food. Fiber is indigestible to dogs because they lack the enzymes necessary to break it down. The percentage of crude fiber is determined by boiling a sample of the dog food in a dilute acid, then in a dilute alkali. This simulates the digestive activities and the gastric secretions of the animal. The residue of this chemical "digestion" process is weighed and ashed (burned). The difference between the initial residue weight and the ash weight indicates the amount of fiber present in the food.

The crude fiber portion actually consists of cellulose, hemicellulose and lignin. Just because there is a fiber content doesn't mean the food is bad for the dog. A small amount of fiber may be beneficial. If the fiber content is too high, though, the food will pass through the animal's system too quickly. When all of the food passes quickly through the system, digestion is less efficient. The food doesn't have enough time to be exposed to all of the digestive enzymes, and the animal doesn't get all of the nutritional benefits.

All of this information lets you look at dog food labels and make some judgements about the food. Compare the guaranteed analysis, list of ingredients, and price. This is only the beginning to finding the best value for your money.

In 1992, a special committee of canine nutrition experts developed new standards for dog and cat food. The Association of American Feed Control Officials (AAFCO) set minimum and maximum requirements for essential nutrients in pet food. To earn the right to use the phrase "complete and balanced," the food must pass a feeding trial conducted with a specified number of dogs following the AAFCO protocol. Alternately it must meet the target levels for these nutrients as stated in the following table. Unfortunately, these can be based on calculations from average analysis of ingredients used in the formula. Not even a chemical analysis of the nutrients in the finished food is required.

This alternative is nothing more or less than an escape clause for those manufacturers who are unwilling to put their products to the ultimate test of "asking the dogs." Regardless of all the other considerations discussed earlier for evaluation and selection of food for your dog, the only one which has real merit is the statement of verification for nutritional adequacy—that is to say, "This food is complete and balanced for all stages of the life cycle (or for growth or maintenance) as substantiated by feeding tests performed in accordance with the procedures established by the Association of American Feed Control Officials (AAFCO)." In other words, look for the key words dog *feeding tests*, or *protocols*, not just the acronym AAFCO. If you don't see the words *feeding tests*, it could mean that just the AAFCO chemical calculation method was used, which tells you less, yet it is better than nothing.

AAFCO Nutrient Profiles for Dog Foods

Nutrient	Units DM Basis	Growth & Repro. Minimum	Adult Maint. Minimum	Maximum
Protein	%	22.0	18.0	
Arginine	%	0.62	0.51	
Histidine	%	0.22	0.18	
Isoleucine	%	0.45	0.37	
Leucine	%	0.72	0.59	
Lysine	%	0.77	0.63	
Methionine-cystine	%	0.53	0.43	
Phenylalanine-tyrosine	%	0.89	0.73	
Threonine	%	0.58	0.48	
Tryptophan	%	0.20	0.16	
Valine	%	0.48	0.39	
Fat	%	8.0	5.0	
Linoleic acid	%	1.0	1.0	
Minerals				
Calcium	%	1.0	0.6	2.5
Phosphorus	%	0.8	0.5	1.6
Ca:P ratio		1:1	1:1	2:1
Potassium	%	0.6	0.6	
Sodium	%	0.3	0.06	

Nutrient	Units DM Basis	Growth & Repro. Minimum	Adult Maint. Minimum	Maximum
Minerals				
Chloride	%	0.45	0.09	
Magnesium	%	0.04	0.04	0.3
Iron	mg/kg	80	80	3000
Copper	mg/kg	7.3	7.3	250
Manganese	mg/kg	5.0	5.0	
Zinc	mg/kg	120	120	1000
Iodine	mg/kg	1.5	1.5	50
Selenium	mg/kg	0.11	0.11	2
Vitamins				
Vitamin A	IU/kg	5000	5000	50000
Vitamin D	IU/kg	500	500	5000
Vitamin E	IU/kg	50	50	1000
Thiamin	mg/kg	1.0	1.0	
Riboflavin	mg/kg	2.2	2.2	
Pantothenic Acid	mg/kg	10	10	
Niacin	mg/kg	11.4	11.4	
Pyridoxine	mg/kg	1.0	1.0	
Folic Acid	mg/kg	0.18	0.18	
Vitamin B-12	mg/kg	0.022	0.022	
Choline	mg/kg	1200	1200	

The units in this table are expressed on a dry matter (DM) basis. Before comparing these levels to those printed on the label of your dog's food, it is necessary to adjust them for the percentage of dry matter (100 − % of water = % of dry matter) the food contains. One way to do this is to take the values given on the label and divide them by the % of DM. The other way is to multiply the table values by the % of DM. (Remember to express percentage as a decimal: 90% = 0.9)

Understanding Dog Food Labels and Literature

Understanding dog food labels allows you to compare one brand with another. A host of terms are on the bags and in manufacturers' advertising and brochures. If you know what they mean, you can evaluate any dog food for its nutrient value and cost.

Many manufacturers use terms that allude to the digestibility of their food. Let's look at how digestion works, what the terms mean and why they're important. Unfortunately, information on digestibility rarely appears on the label.

Digestion is the process where proteins, fats, and carbohydrates are broken down by chemicals and digestive enzymes into smaller subunits that can be absorbed by the body. Proteins are broken into amino acids, fats into fatty acids and triglycerides, and carbohydrates, like starch, into sugars.

Digestive enzymes are organic catalysts that are produced by cells in the body. These enzymes speed the biochemical reactions of digestion at normal body temperature. The enzymes are not used up in the process.

Digestibility

Digestibility refers to the quantity or percentage of the food absorbed in the digestive process from the quantity of the food consumed. The more nutrients which are digested (proteins, fats, carbohydrates, vitamins, minerals), the more will be available and the higher the digestibility figure.

Digestion data measures the disappearance (absorption) of a nutrient as it passes through the gastrointestinal tract. To determine the digestibility of a nutrient, a digestion trial is conducted. The food is analyzed to determine its nutrient content.

The dog is fed a "marker substance" that is inert and nontoxic. Then the dog is fed a specific amount of the food, followed by another marker substance. The feces between markers are collected and analyzed for the undigested nutrient residues of the food consumed. (Urine is not collected or analyzed in a simple digestibility trial.) The difference between total nutrients consumed and total nutrients voided is the quantity apparently digested.

Many animals must be used when determining the digestibility of food. The final figures are averaged from all the animals used in the trial. This is to minimize the variability of results from individual to individual.

Digestibility refers to the relationship between the amount of nutrients consumed with the food and the quantity of those nutrients absorbed by the body. The difference between the two amounts is referred to by nutritionists as the *apparent* coefficient of digestibility. It is called apparent because we do not directly determine the true digestibility of a nutrient.

This coefficient is expressed as a percentage of the food or nutrient that is absorbed. For example, if 10 grams of protein is consumed, and 9.5 grams is absorbed, then the digestibility of this protein would be 95 percent.

The apparent coefficient of digestibility is used for the calculation of digestible crude protein, digestible crude fat, digestible ash and digestible fiber.

Another term used by dog food manufacturers is total dry matter digestibility (TDMD). This literally represents the difference between the food consumed (minus any moisture content) and the food excreted as feces, or the differences between what goes in and what comes out. TDMD in actuality merely tells you how efficiently dogs process the food. It doesn't tell you with any precision what the available or metabolizable energy content of the food really is.

Digestible Energy

Pet food manufacturers measure energy in kilocalories per kilogram and as either digestible energy (DE) or metabolizable energy (ME).

Energy is the primary requirement the food fulfills for the dog. Energy is required for all of the processes involved with growth, lactation, reproduction and physical performance.

Energy is expressed in terms of calories—the amount of energy (heat) required to raise the temperature of one gram of water one degree centigrade. One thousand calories equals 1 kilocalorie (kcal).

It is common to express the caloric content of dog food in terms of kilocalories per kilogram or kilocalories per cup of dog food.

Gross energy is how much energy the food contains. It doesn't tell you anything about the ability of the dog to get that energy out of the food, but when stated as digestible or metabolizable energy, it means you know how the food will perform in the dog.

You may find more precise energy expressions in some brochures, but manufacturers are not permitted to put these on the dog food label until January 1994. (You can always call the manufacturer. Most, but not all, will tell you the DE or ME content.)

Before you can determine the digestible energy of the food, you must determine the total caloric content of the food (gross energy). Gross energy is analytically determined in a laboratory using an instrument known as a bomb calorimeter. Gross energy is the calories (heat) resulting from the complete combustion of the food.

Of course, not all of the gross energy of a food is available to the dog. A certain percentage will not be absorbed and will be passed through and excreted in the feces. When this energy is accounted for, the amount of energy actually absorbed by the animal will be the digestible energy, or DE. It is the actual amount of energy absorbed by the dog. DE information, however, does not account for urine energy and has limited value. What you really want to know is the metabolized energy content (ME)—i.e., what is really available to the dog.

Metabolizable Energy

It's already been stated that not all of the digestible energy can be used by the dog. Some is passed through in the urine. Metabolizable energy takes into account the amount of energy lost in both the feces and the urine. Thus ME gives the most accurate figure regarding the amount of energy available to the dog.

For example, proteins are broken down into a nitrogen substance called urea. Urea cannot be used by the dog and is eliminated in the urine. The amount of energy lost in the urine is 1.25 kcal per gram of protein.

In order to determine the ME, the digestibility of the diet must first be found through feeding trials. The AAFCO pet food committee has written a very specific protocol to do this.

To summarize, metabolizable energy (ME) equals gross food energy minus gross fecal and urinary energy. It is what is really available to your dog and is the best way to compare dog foods. It is not acceptable to compare the ME of one food to the DE of another.

Feeds and Feeding

A dog's nutritional needs vary throughout his life. During the period of life from birth through adolescence, your dog will require twice the energy intake per unit of body weight as that of an adult dog. A pregnant dog may require a moderate increase in food intake during the last two or three weeks of pregnancy. And a nursing dog may require up to a 300 percent increase in energy intake to adequately feed her puppies. That's why many brands of dog food now come in special formulas for growth, adult maintenance, weight control, senior and performance.

In cold weather, expect your dog to eat more. He's burning calories to stay warm, especially if he is spending time outdoors or running through snow.

Heavy exercise such as hunting, racing or herding will also mean higher energy requirements. Heavy exercisers may need as much as twice the maintenance level of energy intake. You can feed a higher protein, higher fat food or simply feed more of the lower protein, lower fat food.

Generally speaking, use the label instructions as a starting point and adjust for your dog's particular needs. If your dog is gaining weight on a food, cut back on the quantity or switch to a lower fat, but not necessarily lower protein, food. The key to selecting the right food is careful observation of the needs of each individual dog.

Evaluating Nutritional Problems

When evaluating nutritional problems in your dog, consider the activity level of the dog, the water content of the diet and what you, the master (feeder), are doing.

More than anything, physiological state and activity level determines the dog's nutritional requirements. A more active dog needs more energy than a less active dog. Active dogs need lots of energy. A drier food will supply more energy per pound than a high moisture food. Growing puppies and pregnant and nursing dogs need more total nutrients and energy than adult dogs. Higher-energy, nutrient-dense foods are preferred for such dogs.

Another big piece of the nutritional picture is you. You can be the best thing for your dog's diet, but more likely you are the worst thing for your dog's nutritional well-being. Are you overindulging your animals with food? Are you subjecting them to careless and haphazard feeding practices, such as giving them table scraps or not giving them a carefully measured portion of food each day? Do you change the dog's food every time another brand is on sale, instead of feeding a consistent diet? Are you feeding the dog on a different schedule every day, instead of on a regular timetable? Are you adding things to the commercial food, which throws the nutritional balance off? See the problem? Your dog doesn't need constant changes in food or feeding schedule. Most commercial diets are carefully formulated, and work just fine. Don't be your dog's worst enemy. Feed a high quality dog food. Be consistent!

Food Allergies

If your dog is itchy all year round or has skin problems all the time, one cause could be a food allergy. Food hypersensitivity is the third most common type of canine allergic disease.

A food allergy can develop after the dog has been eating a food for some time. The more a dog is exposed to the food ingredient, the more sensitive to it the dog becomes. Food hypersensitivity usually shows up early in the dog's life—less than one year of age is common, although it can strike at any age.

Don't confuse food allergies with food poisoning or digestive disorders. The clues to these problems are gastrointestinal symptoms. The dog will vomit or have diarrhea. Allergies, on the other hand, normally are skin related. However, 15% to 20% of the cases show gastrointestinal disturbances. See your veterinarian as soon as the dog shows symptoms.

How to Test for a Food Allergy

After you and your veterinarian rule out the other causes of itching (fleas, pollen, grasses, mites and skin diseases), then you should test different dietary combinations to diagnose a food allergy.

You'll need to run a test for at least a month to reach any conclusions about a particular diet.

You may have heard that one diet or another is "hypoallergenic." Many people, including those who should know better, think it means that this food will not cause allergies. That is not true. Hypoallergenic only means less likely to cause an allergic response.

It is because of the confusion surrounding the term "hypoallergenic" that industry regulators (AAFCO and the FDA) swung into action. They recently required pet food makers to eliminate the word from their labels and literature, unless the health claim could be proven and documented in scientific tests, thus proving the food is nonallergenic.

Thus, no one diet is "hypoallergenic." However, switching to a food containing ingredients that your dog has not previously encountered could eliminate the substance causing the allergic response.

Commercially made lamb- and rice-based dog foods are the currently recognized diets of choice when testing for allergies.

Other new foods on the market that can be used to determine if a food allergy is your dog's problem include canned dog food made with rabbit and rice and venison and rice. Relatively few dogs have encountered these ingredients, so it's a good idea to reserve their use until an allergy develops.

If your dog is on a soy-based food, try a meat- or chicken-based food. If you think wheat or corn is the culprit, find a food with some other grain instead—i.e., rice, barley, or oats.

There are plenty of choices out there. Read the ingredient lists, shop and compare.

For a true food allergy test, select a very different food, such as a lamb and rice diet. Introduce the food over a three-day period, mixing one third the first day with two thirds of the old diet, half and half the second day and two thirds of the new diet the third day, then continue on the new food for thirty days.

As with any good scientific study, you'll want to control any outside variables that could influence your test. Feed your dog from a ceramic or stainless steel dish—not plastic. Plastic bowls are porous and may retain old food residue even after washing.

Do not give any snacks, commercial or otherwise. No table scraps! Don't give your dog rawhide or other toys to chew on. Limit vinyl toys as well. Talk to your veterinarian about possibly restructuring your dog's medication for the duration of the test.

Then keep a daily record of your dog's comfort level. Is he scratching as much? In the same places? Is he pawing his face, rolling on his back, chewing? Has the skin color changed?

If food allergy is the problem, you should see a significant improvement within a month.

To verify that food hypersensitivity was the problem, consult with your veterinarian about putting your dog back on the old diet for two weeks to see if the allergy returns. Make no other changes—keep him away from snacks, etc. If the itching comes back, you'll know for sure it was the food to which your dog was allergic.

If your dog was free of symptoms on the new diet, add back treats and toys one at a time. Watch to see if these are the culprits.

If your dog still has problems on the new diet, see your veterinarian. You and your veterinarian will have to go through a whole new process of elimination to determine which foods your dog can eat safely. If the itching disappears, you're on the right track; if not, try a different food.

If your dog can't tolerate any commercial food and you have found certain human foods he can eat, you may have to start cooking dinner for your dog yourself. Ask your veterinarian how to make a complete and balanced diet from the foods he can eat safely and ask him to recommend which vitamin/mineral tablet you need to use in order to adequately meet your dog's requirements for essential nutrients.

Allergic dogs may be allergic to many things. Food may be only one piece of the puzzle. Your dog may be allergic to flea saliva and/or to pollens or mold. The dog may be able to live with those allergies without major itching. However, if he is also subject to a food sensitivity, this may be too much for his body to handle.

In dogs who have multiple allergies, reducing the contribution of any one factor may lead to measured success. If you eliminate the dog's fleas, then the food allergy may no longer be important.

Don't let your pet suffer. With the help of your veterinarian, seek out the cause of his itchiness and eliminate it. He'll be your best friend forever.

10

Preventive Health Care

A PREVENTIVE HEALTH CARE PROGRAM CAN INCREASE THE quality of your dog's life. It can also decrease the likelihood of your dog's getting a transmissible disease.

An efficient and effective three-part program for preventing many common canine diseases includes vaccinations, medications and a clean environment. Vaccinations help prevent many devastating and often fatal diseases. They're not expensive, and your veterinarian can give them all in a matter of minutes. Most vaccines should be given annually, although puppy vaccinations must be given in a series.

Medications and insecticides help to keep your dog healthy and safe from internal parasites such as heartworms, hookworms, whipworms and tapeworms. By providing a clean, parasite-free environment you can help control the spread of disease. That means disinfecting the place your dog inhabits and keeping the outdoor areas picked up. Fleas should be eliminated from the dog's environment, too, as they lead to skin problems and tapeworms.

Two Main Factors That Affect Your Dog's Health Care Needs

Age and environment play a big part in determining the health care needs of your dog. Vaccinations and fecal examinations are needed more frequently by puppies than by older dogs. Dogs should be checked for internal parasites at least four times a year.

As for environment, certain climates are more conducive to parasite infestations. The southern states have a flea problem that lasts most of the year, while in the more northern states the flea season lasts only a few months. Similarly, mosquitoes breeding year round in a tropical climate mean that heartworm preventive medications must be given all year long.

Health Records

Your veterinarian will keep medical records on your dog. You should, too. Health records help you remember when your dog was vaccinated and for which diseases. Keep a record indicating when you had the dog checked for worms and any prescribed deworming procedures. These records can assist your veterinarian. Keep a record of clinical signs, illnesses, prescribed medication and your dog's reactions and your veterinarian will be able to make a better assessment of recurring problems. Good health records also provide ready information for another veterinarian should you move.

How to Give Your Dog Pills

Some dogs will happily munch pills as though they were treats. Others require a combination of creativity and knowledge to get the pill down the dog's throat.

Here's the basic method to use:

Open your dog's mouth by resting your hand over the bridge of your dog's muzzle, with your wrist on your dog's forehead. Press your thumb in and upward on his lip just behind the canine teeth. Use your fingers to press on the other side of his mouth in the same place. This pressure will cause your dog to open his mouth. Your

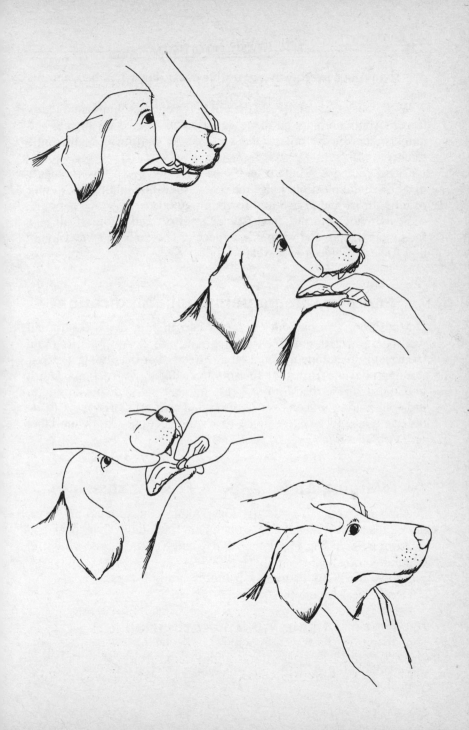

dog should not bite down as you have the dog's lips between his teeth.

With your other hand, hold the pill between your thumb and index finger. Apply pressure on the lower jaw with your other fingers and quickly deposit the pill on the back center portion of your dog's tongue.

Close your dog's mouth and keep it closed for a few moments in a horizontal position. Once the dog has swallowed the pill, gently rub the throat and praise him for being good.

If your dog squirms, have someone else steady him. If all else fails, take the pill and wrap it in a piece of cheese or in some canned dog food and give it as a treat.

Important Reminders About Medication

Medication can play an important part in your dog's health and well-being, but it must be used correctly to do its job. If given incorrectly, medicine may not be as effective or may be dangerous. So, don't deviate from your veterinarian's dosing instructions. Don't give a drug prescribed for one pet to another without checking with the veterinarian first. Never assume that two pills appearing to be the same are, in fact, the same exact medication. Check the label on the bottles!

Warning About Aspirin-Free Analgesics

Aspirin is generally safe for dogs. Aspirin substitutes, however, are not safe for dogs. Acetaminophen (including Tylenol®) and ibuprofen (including Motrin®, Advil®, and Nuprin®) can be harmful or fatal.

Spread the word: Aspirin substitutes can kill dogs and cats.

Choosing a Veterinarian

Thousands of veterinarians are out there, and several are right in your neighborhood. How do you find a veterinarian just right for your dog?

The best way is to ask people with a dog which veterinarian they use, what they like or dislike about the veterinarian and why they use that particular one. Good people to ask are the owners of a local pet food store, groomers, or a boarding kennel operator. All are people with experience with dogs, who know the reputations of the local veterinarians.

The next step is to try the veterinarian. If you don't like one veterinarian's style, try another one. Look for a veterinarian who makes friends with your dog. A good veterinarian should put the patient at ease and put you at ease, too. The veterinarian should explain health conditions, procedures and medications in a way you can understand. He or she should take the time to answer questions without making you feel stupid.

A good veterinarian believes in education and has an office filled with literature. The good ones keep current on new procedures and medications, attend seminars and review plenty of literature to keep up to date. Don't be afraid to ask what the veterinarian does to keep up with what's new in veterinary medicine.

The best veterinarians are always friendly and open toward their patients and are readily available in case of an emergency. Don't wait for an emergency to choose your veterinarian. Make an appointment for a routine examination to get to know your new veterinarian. If you have established a relationship with a veterinarian, it will be easier to be seen when you have an emergency.

Health Care Schedule for Puppies and Dogs

A series of vaccinations are needed to protect against diseases such as distemper, hepatitis, leptospirosis, parainfluenza, canine parvovirus, rabies, coronavirus and Lyme disease.

Most vaccines start at six weeks, and are repeated every three to four weeks until sixteen to twenty weeks of age; rabies is only given at three to four months. Yearly boosters are usually needed to maintain the protection.

Parasite control is an important part of maintaining health for your puppy or dog. Let's look at the enemies. These include external parasites—fleas, ticks, and mites—and internal parasites such as worms.

Most puppies have intestinal worms of some sort. Give your veterinarian fresh fecal samples from your dog to keep an eye on the worm situation and keep it under control. A small sample goes a long way to keeping your dog's internal workings parasite-free.

Preventive Health Care Schedule

Procedure	6–8 Weeks	8–12 Weeks	12–16 Weeks	20 Weeks	6 Months	Yearly
Fecal Exam	X	X	X		X	X
Heartworm Test					X	X
Vaccination						
Canine Distemper	X	X	X			X
Infectious Canine Hepatitis	X	X	X			X
Leptospirosis	X	X	X			X
Parvovirus	X	X	X	X*		X
Parainfluenza	X	X	X			X
Coronavirus		X	X			X
Lyme Disease			X	X		X
Canine Cough		X				X
Rabies			X			X⁺

Most veterinarians recommend puppy vaccinations every 4 weeks starting at 6–8 weeks, with the last vaccination given at 16 weeks.

*Parvovirus vaccination is recommended for some breeds (particularly Dobermans and Rottweilers) at 20 weeks of age.

⁺Check with your state regulations.

Vaccinations/Immunizations—How They Work

We've talked several times already about the importance of routine vaccinations/immunizations for the control of infectious diseases. By now you should realize that every dog, puppy or adult, should be adequately immunized (vaccinated) against infectious diseases. Here's an explanation of how vaccines work in people and dogs.

The term "vaccine" has come to mean all types of biological agents used to produce active immunity—they stimulate the body's immune system to protect against a specific infection.

Vaccinations vary in the amount of immunity they create, based on the number and timing of the immunizations, the dose and the specific characteristics of each vaccine. To understand the protection that vaccinations give, you must first understand some basics about the immune system.

How the Immune System Works

The immune system is the part of the body responsible for fighting off attacks from viruses, bacteria or other infectious agents.

The dog's ability to respond to a disease or a vaccine rests principally in the T-cells and B-cells of the lymphoid system. B-cells are responsible for antibody production. T-cells do many things, including stimulating B-cells to produce antibodies.

The immune response involves both functioning B-cells and T-cells. A vaccine works by safely encouraging an immune response that will be effective against a specific disease. The body thinks the vaccine is the disease and creates an antibody to combat the attacker.

Antibodies are specialized proteins (immunoglobulins) secreted by mature B-cells in response to an antigen—any substance the body recognizes as foreign. Antibodies are specifically designed to react with the antigen that stimulated their production in the first place.

How the antibodies behave is determined by their physical, chemical and immunological properties. There are five classes of antibodies, each with a different function:

IgA (Ig stands for immunoglobulin) is present in external secretions such as tears, saliva, milk and the mucosa of the respiratory system. Its production is stimulated by an antigen coming in contact with it, not by a vaccine or infection circulating throughout the body.

IgE is the antibody responsible for allergic reactions.

IgM is the first antibody formed in response to an antigen. It is first on the scene and doesn't live long. If the body only made IgMs, your protection against an antigen would be short-lived. IgG is late on the scene, but confers long-lasting immunity. IgD has not been proven to have any antibody activity. When an animal or human is immunized (vaccinated) for the first time in its life, IgM production begins immediately, peaking within a few days and disappearing, leaving no permanent protection. IgG production starts just prior to the IgM peak level of production.

When an animal is later immunized for a second time with the same or similar antigen (a booster shot), there is a quicker and higher level of antibody production, with the immunity lasting longer than the first time. IgM production may be similar, but IgG formation is far greater than the first time. (See chart on page 132.)

This is why a series of shots is important—each immunization in a series increases antibody production and gives long-lasting immunity. Don't skip any booster shots!

A vaccination isn't foolproof. It can be overpowered, resulting in the dog (or person) getting the infectious disease despite being vaccinated. This can be caused by massive exposure to a virus, contact with a mutated or highly virulent strain, high stress, poor sanitary conditions or a combination of the above factors.

How Sanitation Works with Vaccinations to Protect Your Dog

Good sanitary and animal husbandry techniques are designed to limit exposure to infectious organisms. Vaccinations work together with good sanitary practices to make one comprehensive, effective system of protection. You can't have full protection without both vaccination and sanitation.

Here's an example. The dogs in Boho's Kennel have canine cough, which has multiple causes including bacteria (bordatella), viruses (parainfluenza virus and adenovirus) and mycoplasmas.

Despite warnings from the owner of Boho's Kennel, John Doe continually comes to visit for a cup of coffee and chitchat. John Doe returns home and plays with his healthy dog.

When John Doe visits next, Boho's Kennel's owner again warns, "Don't come over, my dogs are sick." John Doe brushes off the warning. "It's all right, my dog is vaccinated," he says and continues to return for his daily coffee and gossip session.

Unknown to John Doe is the fact that canine cough is spread through respiratory secretions. The causative agents spread through the air in tiny droplets every time an infected dog coughs. Airborne droplet infections saturate everything in the environment where dogs have been coughing: furniture, floors, clothes and walls, among other things.

On each visit to Boho's Kennel, droplets cling to John Doe and he brings more of the agents back to his house. After two weeks the dogs at Boho's Kennel have recuperated, but now John Doe's dog is sick.

How did it happen? On every visit, John Doe increased the population of the causative agents in his own house. Finally the dog couldn't tolerate the massive exposure, and the agents overpowered any protection given by the vaccine.

The disease spread further when John Doe visited his other dog-owning neighbor as he brought more and more of the agents with him—the cycle starts all over again.

Passive Immunity

In humans, antibodies are transferred to the fetus through the placenta. In dogs, this antibody transfer occurs in the first twenty-four hours of life through the colostrum, or premilk from the dam (mother).

Colostrum contains a very high concentration of all the dam's antibodies. These are readily absorbed through the newborn's intestinal tract and protect the puppy. This is called passive immunity—immunity that is transferred.

It's important that as much of the passive immunity as possible be transferred. It is absolutely imperative that the newborn pup be given the dam's colostrum as soon as possible. Without antibodies, the puppy is susceptible to every infection present in the environment.

The puppy's ability to absorb the antibodies from colostrum diminishes after twenty-four hours. Make sure all puppies nurse on the dam. The puppy now has the antibodies the dam has made.

If at five or six weeks the puppy still has a large number of

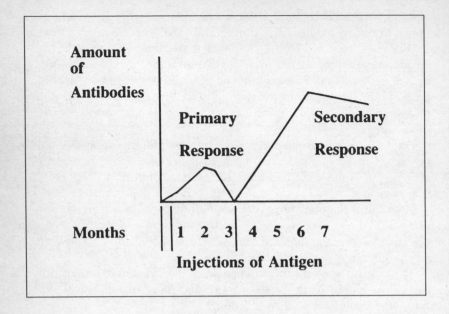

maternal antibodies circulating in its system, it will not be able to produce its own antibodies.

The maternal antibodies can interfere with the immunization of your puppy as late as sixteen weeks of age. By having a series of shots over time, you increase the likelihood that the puppy is protected—even if the early shots were subject to interference by the maternal antibodies.

Diseases

What Is a Disease?

A disease is any abnormal condition with readily visible symptoms. Each disease has its own set of symptoms. For example, diarrhea isn't normally a sign of canine cough, but it could be a sign of parvovirus, coronavirus, salmonella or distemper.

The Two Varieties of Disease

Infectious (contagious) diseases are caused by various types of microorganisms—viruses, bacteria and parasites. Some examples are rabies, parainfluenza, canine cough, parvovirus, brucellosis and ringworm.

Noninfectious diseases are caused by genetic abnormalities and environmental conditions. Environmental conditions include injuries, improper nutrition, and exposure to hazardous materials. Examples of noninfectious diseases include vitamin and mineral deficiencies, lead poisoning and hip dysplasia.

Each infecting organism has its own method of spreading. Some use droplets that are coughed or sneezed. Others are spread by insects, infected feces or contaminated food or water. For example, canine cough is a disease that is spread through airborne droplets coughed into the environment, while canine heartworm and Lyme disease use insects as carriers. Food poisoning bacteria will contaminate feed if permitted to grow, and single-cell protozoans like giardia can contaminate water. Parvovirus is spread in infected feces.

Infectious organisms frequently "catch a ride" from one dog to another. They may be picked up by the dog's hair or feet, or transmitted by your shoes, grooming equipment, food and water bowls, trash cans, dog crates or dog runs.

Most people think that the only way your dog can be exposed to disease is to be directly exposed to a sick dog. As you can see, that isn't the only way for disease to spread. Anything that comes in contact with the sick dog or that comes in contact with infectious organisms shed by sneezing, coughing or defecating may spread the disease. If you have a sick dog, automatically assume that everything the dog has been near is contaminated and proceed to disinfect all of those surfaces and objects.

The People Problem

The biggest factor in transmitting canine disease is people. A person pets a dog, picking up bacteria and viruses and then plays with another dog who would not ordinarily have contact with the infected animal. The second dog gets the disease, too. Sometimes we carry disease from kennel to kennel on our hands, our clothing and, especially, our shoes.

You can take steps to reduce transmission of disease. If you own a kennel, make sure visitors and kennel help disinfect the soles of their shoes before entering the kennel. Make a shoe bath by placing a shallow baking pan with a layer of antiseptic or disinfectant solution by the door. Anyone entering or leaving the kennel should cleanse the soles of their shoes. That way they won't bring anything in or take anything nasty home with them! (Be sure no animal can drink or step in the shoe bath.)

Visitors and kennel help should be required to wear disposable or washable coveralls, smocks or aprons—especially if there is illness in your kennel. Many microorganisms ride on clothing in their search for a new dog to infect.

Always wash your hands before and after handling other dogs. Hand contact is a major way disease is spread between people, as well as dogs.

Any dog brought into your home or kennel should be fully vaccinated. It may seem simple, but it works. This should be done at least two weeks before to build an immune response. Isolate the newcomer for a week or two and watch for signs of illness.

When it comes to disease, dog shows create special concerns. Dog-to-dog contact is common, and person/dog/dog contact is also common. Because many diseases are spread through the feces, you can decrease the chance of bringing diseases home with a spray disinfectant such as Lysol®. Carry a can with you and spray the bottoms of your shoes as you get in or out of your truck, car or van.

If your dog has ringworm, which is caused by a fungus, you may inadvertently spread the fungus from one dog to another by using the same grooming tools. The solution is simple: disinfect your grooming equipment between dogs.

Remember Legionnaires' disease? This bacterial infection was spread through air conditioning systems and killed many people. Filters can catch large debris in which bacteria may be riding, although they won't catch free-floating bacteria or any other small microorganisms. Change your air conditioning or furnace filters at least monthly.

Diseases of Dogs

Viruses

Viruses are the smallest infectious agent. They consist of a shell made of protein, filled with genetic material. Each virus contains only one kind of genetic material, DNA or RNA. Viruses are inert, or inactive, outside of a living body. They enter the host wherever they can and produce disease elsewhere in the body.

Viruses are parasites on the cellular level. They replicate (multiply) only in living cells. Some viruses are very specific in their targets. They may infect only certain species or certain groups of species or specific types of cells within a particular animal. For example, some viruses only infect dogs, while rabies can infect any warm-blooded animal, including man.

To produce disease, viruses must enter a host, come in contact with the specific, susceptible cells the virus is after and then replicate. The virus often destroys the cells when it releases all of the newly replicated viruses. Destruction of the cells in the target tissues and the body's response to the cell and tissue injury is responsible for the development of the disease.

Viruses enter their host through the mucosa (mucous membranes) of the respiratory system. They can also enter through the gastrointestinal tract, by an insect bite or by being introduced directly into the bloodstream by needles. Hepatitis B and HIV are examples of viruses that can be transmitted through contaminated needles.

Parvovirus

In 1978, dogs of all ages and breeds became victims of a highly contagious viral disease called canine parvovirus (CPV). Parvovirus attacks the intestinal tract, white blood cells and occasionally the dog's heart muscle.

Parvovirus is spread from dog to dog through feces. Large amounts of the virus are shed from the intestinal tract into the feces. The virus is extremely resistant to adverse environmental conditions and can survive for long periods of time. Parvovirus is readily transmitted from place to place on your shoe bottoms, the hair on your dog's feet and any other object that comes in contact with the contaminated feces. It is a dog-exclusive disease and cannot be transmitted to other types of animals or people.

Symptoms of Parvovirus.   The first signs of parvovirus appear within one week of the dog coming into contact with infected feces. The dog will vomit or have severe diarrhea. The feces will be light gray or yellow gray or liquid and streaked with blood. The dog may suffer from dehydration as a result of the vomiting and diarrhea. Other symptoms include depression, loss of appetite and fever of 104 to 106 degrees Fahrenheit in puppies (less in older dogs).

As the disease becomes more serious, dogs may vomit repeatedly. The diarrhea may become bloody and projectile, spurting out. The white blood cell count will drop, and the dog will die within forty-eight to seventy-two hours of the onset of clinical signs.

The majority of unvaccinated puppies less than five months old who contract parvovirus die. In older dogs the mortality rate is much less.

Diagnosis and Treatment of Parvovirus.   A veterinarian will make the diagnosis based on the history, clinical signs, hematology and results of tests that detect parvovirus in the feces. Because there are no specific drugs that kill the virus, treatment consists mainly of supportive care. The dog must be placed on intravenous fluids to ensure that the hydration status is properly maintained. Intravenous antibiotics are given to prevent secondary bacterial sepsis, and other supportive measures (anti-vomiting drugs, blood transfusions, etc.) are used if indicated. The dog should have nothing to eat or drink until the vomiting has stopped for twenty-four hours. At this time, a bland diet may be fed in small amounts for multiple feedings.

Prevention and Protection from Parvovirus.   While parvovirus isn't readily treatable, it is preventable. All dogs should be vaccinated against canine parvovirus (CPV). Proper cleaning and disinfecting of kennels and other areas where an infected dog has been are an absolute necessity to keep the disease from spreading. Picking up after your dog and disinfecting your shoes can help keep parvovirus at bay. A simple solution of one part household chlorine bleach to thirty parts water is an effective disinfectant to use on an area once the feces have been removed. Several heavy-duty disinfectants are now sold that kill parvovirus and other agents that cause disease.

Canine Distemper

Canine distemper is another highly contagious viral disease. It's most often transmitted through contact with an infected dog's mucous secretions or nasal discharge. However, it can also be spread by direct contact with an infected dog's bodily secretions. In the proper environmental conditions, the distemper virus can live for many months.

Symptoms of distemper may include cold-like symptoms with a fever, mucous congestion, bronchitis, gastroenteritis, squinting, eye discharge, poor appetite and listlessness.

Distemper also causes damage by attacking the nervous system of the dog. This is occasionally seen with the initial symptoms, but most commonly these signs occur weeks after apparent recovery from the acute phase of the disease. The following neurologic signs can be exhibited: nervous twitching, chewing gum seizures, circling, ataxia, blindness and convulsions.

Diagnosis and Treatment of Canine Distemper. As with parvovirus, diagnosis is based on history, clinical signs and hematology. A test can be done on cells collected from the conjunctiva or mucous membranes that will detect distemper virus in these cells. Treatment is similar to that used for parvovirus. Vaccination is the best preventive against distemper.

Rabies

All warm-blooded animals, including man, are susceptible to rabies. Most rabies cases in the United States are found in raccoons, skunks and other animals that inhabit the woods.

Today, rabies is as major a threat as it was in the 1930s. Back then rabies was referred to as the "Mad Dog Scare." Today, most states require dogs be vaccinated against rabies. Many even recommend that dairy cattle, horses and other domestic livestock be vaccinated, too.

There are three clinical stages that must be recognized: prodromal, excitatory and paralytic. The prodromal stage is characterized by a change of behavior. Wild animals may let you approach them or will appear at abnormal times during the day. Dogs that are normally friendly and outgoing will become fearful and apprehensive. This stage could last several days and is followed by the excitatory stage. During the excitatory phase, animals may become hyperreactive to various stimuli in their environment. Dogs may attack and bite for no apparent reason; hence this is known as the "mad dog" phase. Other animals will not become hyperreactive, but may become oblivious to their surroundings. This is known as the "dumb" phase. This phase usually lasts three to four days and is followed by the paralytic stage. During the paralytic stage, animals may exhibit paralysis of the muscles in their throat, which leads to the inability to swallow. These animals may appear to be "frothing" at the mouth. As this phase progresses, animals may become completely paralyzed, which is followed by death due to the inability to breathe. This stage will usually last two to three days. Animals that are infected with the rabies virus will usually die within ten days of the onset of clinical signs. Don't ever approach a dog or wild animal that is exhibiting strange or aggressive behavior. If you suspect that the animal is rabid, immediately call your animal control officer. If you are bitten by a strange dog or wild animal, contact your doctor and the animal control officer immediately!

There is no cure for rabies if left untreated, and very few animals and people survive. The disease can be prevented through vaccination.

Infectious Canine Hepatitis (ICH)

Infectious canine hepatitis is a disease caused by an adenovirus that can affect dogs of any age. It is transmitted by ingesting the virus, which is present in the urine and feces of infected dogs. The virus initially infects the tonsils and lymph nodes, then moves to other organs, including the liver and kidneys. The virus ultimately may localize in the kidneys, where it is shed into the urine. The virus can even be passed in the urine and feces several months after the dog has recovered from the disease.

Infectious canine hepatitis has an incubation period of five to seven days. The first signs are an elevated temperature—around 104 degrees Fahrenheit—which lasts from one to six days. The fever may drop and spike back up again. During this initial period, the dog may become depressed, lethargic or anorexic. In prolonged cases, the dog may exhibit the following symptoms: reluctance to move, abdominal tenderness, enlarged tonsils, coughing, bloody diarrhea, increased thirst and urination.

Diagnosis, Treatment and Prevention of ICH. The diagnosis is made by examining the history, clinical signs, blood work and rising antibody titers. As with the other viral diseases, treatment is symptomatic, providing supportive care as needed. The disease can be prevented through vaccination.

Leptospirosis

Leptospirosis is a bacterial disease that infects dogs of all ages. The bacteria is shed in the urine. Most dogs are infected by coming in contact with contaminated food, soil or water, or contaminated urine. Clinical signs include anorexia, vomiting, fever, bloody diarrhea, jaundice, muscle stiffness, abdominal pain, increased thirst and urination, patchy gums that appear blood tinged, labored breathing and depression.

Diagnosis, Treatment and Prevention of Leptospirosis. The diagnosis is made by examining the history, clinical signs, blood work and rising antibody titers. Treatment includes large doses of antibiotics, as well as symptomatic therapy. The disease can be prevented through vaccination.

Because leptospirosis is a disease that can affect humans, care must be taken when handling contaminated materials, and the premises must be properly disinfected.

Canine Coronavirus

Canine coronavirus is a disease that can affect dogs of all ages. Its principal clinical sign is diarrhea. It is very contagious and can spread rapidly through kennels.

Diagnosis, Treatment and Prevention of Canine Coronavirus.
The diagnosis is based on history, clinical signs and blood work.
As with the other viral diseases, therapy consists of supportive
care—most cases recover spontaneously. The disease can be prevented through vaccination.

Canine Cough

Officially, this disease is called infectious tracheobronchitis, and
it is caused by several viruses (particularly parainfluenza virus and
adenovirus), bacteria (*Bordatella bronchiseptica*) and mycoplasma.
The disease is spread primarily through respiratory secretions and
is usually seen in dogs that have been recently kenneled. Dogs with
canine cough usually have a dry, hacking cough.

Diagnosis, Treatment and Prevention of Canine Cough. Diagnosis is based primarily on history and clinical signs. Treatment is
symptomatic, with use of antibiotics for secondary bacterial infections and cough suppressants for severe coughs. Prevention is
through vaccination.

Lyme Disease

This is a hot topic in veterinary medicine. It is caused by a
spirochete, which is transmitted by an Ixodes tick (commonly known
as a deer tick). Clinical signs include fever, lethargy, joint pain,
reluctance to move and depression. In more chronic cases heart,
kidney and neurologic manifestations have been seen.

Diagnosis, Treatment and Prevention of Lyme Disease. Diagnosis
is based on history, clinical signs, elevated antibodies and response
to treatment. Please note that the antibody response is variable,
which often makes this test difficult to interpret by your veterinarian.
Most cases respond to antibiotics, which are given for two to four
weeks. Prevention includes decreasing the risk to tick exposure by
using tick sprays or flea and tick collars, as well as checking the
dogs for ticks after they have been outside. There is a new Lyme
vaccine, which is recommended for use in endemic areas.

This disease is very controversial, and more research needs to be done to more clearly define the clinical aspects of the disease.

Parasites

Now that we've discussed viruses and immunity, let's go on to another common problem of dogs: parasites.

A parasite is an organism that resides on or within another living organism, called the host. A parasite needs a host to find the environment and nutrients it requires for growth and reproduction. Parasites can be both internal and external.

Internal Parasites

Most puppies have worms. Adult dogs occasionally get them, too. With the proper treatment, most worms are not a serious threat to your dog's health. However, they can become serious if they are not kept under control.

All dogs should be checked for worms at least four times a year. A small fecal sample is all the veterinarian needs to check for an infestation of worms. The veterinarian will check the fecal sample for eggs passed by the female worms. Because the worms are often intermittent shedders (they shed their eggs at different times), your veterinarian will ask you to bring in multiple samples taken on different days to diagnose the problem. Worms sap the dog's vitality and health, can cause skin problems and can even cause death in puppies who are heavily infested.

Treating worms properly is simple, but important. Using the incorrect deworming medication will not eliminate the infestation problem. Using the wrong dose of deworming medication can also lead to death. Deworming medicines are poisonous, as the object of deworming the dog is to poison the worms without poisoning the dog.

Don't try to diagnose the type of worms your dog may or may not have. Deworming medications are not to be fooled with. Take a small fecal sample to your veterinarian and have it checked. He'll give you the correct deworming medicine and the correct dose for your dog.

Types of Worms

Ascarids—Roundworms.   Ascarids, or roundworms, are the worms most commonly found in both puppies and adult dogs. Luckily, they are also the most easily removed. Roundworms live in the dog's intestinal tract, where they interfere with digestion and absorption of nutrients, leaving very little to sustain the dog.

Roundworms are a whitish-yellow color and measure from two to eight inches long when not curled up. They frequently can be seen in the puppy's feces, where they look like spaghetti. The immature form can migrate from the stomach to the lungs, where it is often coughed up and swallowed, eventually reaching its ultimate destination, the small intestine. While the larvae migrate through the lungs, the dog may exhibit a soft cough, or in severe cases, pneumonia.

The larvae (immature form) may also lay dormant in the tissues of a female dog. When the dog becomes pregnant, these larvae can awake and infect the fetuses across the placenta. The larvae can also migrate to the mammary glands, where they can infect the puppies through the milk.

A puppy with roundworms may have a potbellied appearance. These puppies often look unthrifty, with a dull hair coat and dull-looking eyes. Other signs to look for are diarrhea, vomiting, listlessness and weight loss.

Roundworms are a less serious problem for adult dogs, as some may develop an immunity to these worms. Stool samples should be checked anyway, as a precautionary measure.

Whipworms.   Whipworms pass their eggs in the feces, where the larvae develop inside the egg. These eggs can potentially infect your dog. Whipworm eggs are very resistant to the environment, so they may survive in the soil for long periods of time.

Dogs become infected when they swallow an infective egg picked up from the ground, either from licking their feet or from contaminated food or water. Symptoms of whipworm infestation include a chronic foul-smelling diarrhea, often flecked with blood, abdominal pain, unthriftiness and occasional periods of constipation.

Whipworms are often difficult to treat, usually requiring multiple treatments with worm medication. Not only must you treat your dog, but you must decontaminate the environment to prevent reinfestation.

Hookworms.   Hookworms produce some of the same clinical signs as roundworms; however, their primary importance is in their ability to cause anemia. Hookworms are bloodsuckers that can cause exsanguination in the most severe cases. Puppies are commonly infected by ingesting larvae in the dam's milk. In severe cases, these puppies can rapidly deteriorate. They often have soft to liquid feces, which are dark in color because the blood is partially digested.

Adult dogs are infected in one of two ways. In most cases, the dogs ingest the infective larvae, who migrate to the small intestine. Alternatively, hookworm eggs may hatch outdoors within twelve to twenty-four hours if the temperature and environment are optimal. The larvae can penetrate the dog's skin, migrate through the body and reach the small intestines, where they develop into adults.

Sanitation is vital to controlling hookworms. Once your dogs have become infested with hookworms, you must take care to kill the eggs and larvae on the ground. In most cases, a good hard freeze will solve the problem. However, in warmer climates, a 1 percent solution of chlorine bleach can be used on paved surfaces and cages. Sodium borate can be used on gravel-surfaced dog runs. Liming, or in *extreme* cases, burning your lawn will help control the hookworm in these areas. There are some other chemicals that can help to control hookworm in the environment—consult your veterinarian.

Tapeworms.   Tapeworms are a common internal parasite of dogs. They do not affect the health of the dog as noticeably as other worms. Tapeworms come in at least fourteen different species and vary in size from an inch to several feet in length. Tape worms are transmitted by fleas, lice, rodents and rabbits. These intermediate hosts are necessary for the tapeworm to complete its life cycle.

Tapeworm segments are passed in the dog's feces. The segments rupture, releasing eggs to all areas of the dog's environment.

Flea larvae, who are also living in the environment, feed on the tapeworm eggs. When the flea larvae mature, they jump on the dog for their blood meal. The dog, irritated by the fleas, bites, scratches and chews at the irritated area. Eventually, the dog eats one of the fleas, which is carrying the tapeworm larvae.

As the ingested flea moves through the digestive tract, the immature tapeworm is released and grows to adulthood. In the intestine, the adult tapeworm attaches to the intestinal wall, where it matures and ultimately passes new egg-filled segments, which repeat the cycle all over again.

Symptoms of tapeworm infestation in dogs include digestive disturbances and a generally unhealthy appearance. You may see small segments of the worms in the dog's feces, or dried segments which look like grains of rice on the fur under the tail. Your dog may also drag his hindquarters on the floor or ground, although this is most commonly a symptom of blocked anal glands.

Treatment for tapeworms is specifically designed for tapeworms. One dose of pills usually does the trick. It's important to rid the dog and his living area of the intermediate host, such as the flea, so that reinfestation does not occur.

Protozoal Organisms.   Protozoa are single-celled microorganisms. Many types may live in the dog, including giardia and four species of coccidia. Giardia and coccidia inhabit the mucous membrane lining of the small intestine and the colon.

Dogs suffering from giardia will have diarrhea, flatulence and an unthrifty appearance. Giardia can be detected microscopically by looking at a direct smear of the feces. More commonly, however, giardia is detected by performing a fecal flotation and observing the cysts microscopically. Typically, giardia is picked up by drinking water contaminated by fecal matter from infected animals. Giardia can also be transmitted to humans. Proper sanitation and disinfection must be used if your dog has giardia.

Coccidiosis, an infestation of coccidia, can be detected only under the microscope and is one of the most troublesome parasitic diseases of puppies and young dogs. Acute cases of coccidia may show symptoms similar to distemper. Proper sanitation is of the utmost importance in controlling coccidiosis, which is usually seen in crowded, unsanitary conditions. Cleaning the dog's environment is mandatory to prevent reinfestation—just as it is with other parasites.

Coccidiosis has little impact on adult dogs. The adult can be a carrier, though, and spread the organisms to other dogs. In most cases, the mother is the source of infection of a litter. Coccidiosis is usually seen in puppies when they are about a month old, especially in poorly raised puppies. Occasionally it is seen in otherwise healthy puppies following traumatic stress.

The most common sign of coccidiosis is a mucoid diarrhea, occasionally with specks of blood. In some cases, the diarrhea may become so severe that the puppies will become dehydrated. These puppies may cough, have a discharge from the eyes and nose, and develop a slight fever. It is important that puppies receive immediate veterinary care to prevent further dehydration and death. Along with treatment, the environment must be decontaminated to prevent coccidial infection in other puppies.

Heartworm. Heartworms are deadly internal parasites that are found in the right side of the heart and its associated vessels. There are two types of blood tests that can detect either the microfilariae (the immature form) or the adult worms. Most veterinarians can quickly do these tests in their offices.

The heartworms are transmitted by the bite of an infected mosquito. Larvae travel in the bloodstream and mature in the heart. At eight to fourteen inches, the adult heartworm clogs the right heart chambers and major blood vessels and can break off and cause problems in the lungs. They can damage the heart and other organs before any symptoms are visible. In its advanced stages, heartworm infestation will cause coughing, labored breathing, uncommon weakness, ascites (fluid in the abdomen), and eventually, heart failure and death.

Heartworm infestations require a long series of treatments to kill the adult heartworms without clogging important blood vessels around the heart. It's far easier and safer to prevent heartworms than to treat them. Several preventatives are on the market today. After the blood test shows your dog to be free of heartworm larvae, you can give your dog a pill once a month or once a day, beginning a month prior to mosquito season. These pills must be continued through the first frost. If you live in a tropical area where mosquitoes are a problem most of the year, you'll want to give the pills all year long. Some of the pills are chewable or available in a medicated treat (Heartgard®).

Prevention of Internal Parasites

Control and prevention of internal parasites is aimed at breaking one phase of their life cycle. Clean living conditions and prompt diagnosis are important for keeping reinfestation to a minimum.

Keep the dog's environment free of fleas, lice and mosquitoes. Floors, kennel runs and yards should be kept clean, with feces removed at least once a day. Drinking water, food bowls and other utensils should be washed daily. Runs should be scrubbed and hosed with a germicide to ensure all unwanted microbes and parasites are killed. (Remember to remove the dogs and their food bowls when using harsh chemicals.) Bedding should be cleaned and changed regularly.

Worm eggs and larvae, if not killed, will continually reinfest the dog. Fecal samples should be examined by a veterinarian seasonally, with treatment and clean-up action taken promptly to prevent reinfestation.

Never worm a dog who is weak or sick without the advice of a veterinarian. Deworming medicines are poison, so do not administer them needlessly!

If you have a sick dog, you must also disinfect all possible sources of contamination—including floors, walls, ceilings, fences, crates, water bowl and grooming equipment. Wash your clothes and disinfect your shoes, too, to keep down the population of microorganisms.

Please Note: Hookworms, roundworms, giardia, and in some rare cases, tapeworms can be transmitted to people. Please consult your veterinarian concerning this potential public health problem.

External Parasites

External parasites live on the outside of your dog. Most every dog gets fleas and ticks now and then. They are a natural part of a dog's environment, so their presence is not a reflection on you or your living habits.

Fleas and ticks are extremely irritating to your dog and can lead to serious skin disorders and disease. These external parasites are difficult to get rid of unless you follow a set treatment schedule.

Many times fleas and ticks go undetected until they are present in great numbers. Keep an eye on your dog. If you find him scratching, biting or chewing himself, or if you find a bald spot, chances are your dog is infested with some sort of external parasite.

Fleas

By far, the flea is the most annoying pest faced by your dog, as it is difficult to eliminate and can drive both you and your dog crazy.

To eliminate fleas from your dog, you must control the little guys in three areas: on the dog, in the living quarters (his and yours) and in the outdoor environment where your dog spends time.

Control of fleas in the inside environment can be accomplished in one of three ways. The easiest way to control indoor fleas is to hire an exterminator to fumigate your house. Be sure to tell them that you have a flea problem. The second form of flea control involves spraying the house with a trigger spray. This is very labor intensive, but good results can be achieved if done properly. The final way to control fleas in your house involves setting off aerosol bombs. This is less labor intensive than the trigger spray, but must be done properly to achieve the right results. The most common failure with this form of treatment is not buying enough bombs to adequately cover the entire house.

Flea eggs are very resistant to many adverse environmental conditions, and they are difficult to kill. Because of this, many products contain insect growth regulators that prevent the larvae from becoming adult fleas. These products help to break the life cycle of the flea and thus prevent them from setting up in your house. Consult your exterminator or veterinarian about these products.

No matter how you control the fleas in the house, *always read the label and follow instructions carefully*.

Use caution when combining different flea products. It may be unwise to use a flea collar, shampoo, dip and powder all at once. Flea products are poisonous chemicals, especially if used in certain combinations. Consult your veterinarian if you have a question about combining certain products.

The most common flea control on the dog is a shampoo and dip combination. Most flea shampoos kill only those fleas currently on the dog; they often have very little residual value. Dips, on the other hand, are not usually rinsed off, and can provide a residual value of up to three weeks, repelling or even killing the fleas. Many veterinarians will even have you spray the dog a few days after the shampoo/dip, depending on the level of infestation. Consult your veterinarian about this aggressive form of flea control.

There are hundreds of other products on the market for controlling fleas. These include pills, powders, insecticides that can be applied every two weeks, ultrasonic collars and herbal remedies. Herbal products, usually based on pennyroyal, eucalyptus and rosemary, may have some flea-repelling properties. Consult your veterinarian to determine the right product to control the fleas on your dog.

One of the insecticides that is derived from plant materials is pyrethrin. Pyrethrin is a chemical synthesized from pyrethrum (chrysanthemum) flowers. This is a naturally occurring substance that quickly kills fleas. Products that contain pyrethrins will usually kill the fleas on the animal within hours. Pyrethrin is unstable in light, and does not have a residual value of more than a day or two. Permethrin is a man-made version, which won't lose its effectiveness as quickly when exposed to sunlight. It thus offers a longer residual effect.

Finally, flea control must be performed outside, where the dog is allowed to roam. Outside sprays are used to control the fleas in the yard.

Bald Spots

Bald spots can be caused by a dog chewing at flea-irritated skin, a fungal infection, lice or mites. If your dog has a bald spot take him to the veterinarian for proper diagnosis and treatment.

Ticks

Ticks are the hardiest external parasite. They lie in wait for victims in bushes, leaves, tall grass and undergrowth. Look for ticks daily on your dog during warm weather, especially on the ears, head, neck, between the toes, and in the folds between the legs and body. Tick removal isn't difficult, but it can be tricky. You must remove the entire tick, including the head embedded in your dog's skin. If you do not get the entire tick, you'll run the risk of infection.

Here's how to remove a tick. First, don't even think of using a match on your dog. Instead, take a cotton swab, dip it in some alcohol and gently stroke the tick until the tick has become soaked in the alcohol. After a few strokes, the tick will usually loosen its hold on the dog. With a pair of good tweezers, gently remove the tick. Please remember that ticks carry disease that can be transmitted to humans. Do not use your fingers to remove the tick from the dog.

If the tick does not remove easily, then its head is still embedded in your dog's skin. Ticks are very stubborn, and it may take a few more strokes with the alcohol-soaked cotton swab to get it to come peacefully. Never attempt this procedure around your dog's eyes. If your dog has a tick embedded in his eyelid, let the veterinarian remove it.

The best prevention is to dip or spray your dog regularly, as you would for fleas. Remember to always follow the manufacturer's directions.

Lice

Dog lice are a health threat to young puppies. Lice are so small they are not usually discernible to the human eye. While not as common as fleas or other external parasites, lice are bloodsuckers and can cause anemia in puppies and weakness in adults.

A few lice can make a dog itchy, but with thousands of them, the dog may not scratch at all. Lice can penetrate the dog's skin and suck blood. Female lice then lay eggs on the dog, which in about twenty-one days hatch and develop into adult lice.

If you think your dog has lice, see your veterinarian.

Mites and Mange

Mange is caused by another type of external parasite, mites. Mites are also not discernible to the human eye. They are rarely seen in well-fed and cared-for dogs. Mites can be present any time during the year.

Two common types of mange are seen in dogs: red mange, also known as dermodectic mange, and sarcoptic mange, also known as scabies. Dogs suffering from red mange do not usually scratch. Red mange is seen more often in short-haired dogs and begins in small areas of hairlessness. The bald spot can be reddish in color, accompanied by an irritated appearance.

Sarcoptic mange causes severe itching with subsequent skin irritation and hair loss. It is contagious to people. If you suspect mange, have your veterinarian take a small scraping of the dog's irritated bald spot and check it under the microscope for the organism. Several skin scrapings may be necessary—mites are elusive little creatures.

Mange is a serious skin disease that, if untreated, can lead to severe skin infections. Mange is treated by clipping the infested area and using medicated baths or sprays and oral medication.

Ear Mites

Ear mites are another external parasite that is an annoyance to dogs. Mites are quite common and spend most of their life in the dog's ear. Often the dog is infected long before any signs of their existence are visible.

Ear mites are very irritating to the dog. Signs of ear mites are scratching until bleeding sores appear around his ears. You may also see a reddish-brown, waxy substance deep in the dog's ear. This waxy substance, a mixture of blood, ear wax and dirt, is noticeably thicker than the dirt that is normally present as a thin layer around the entire ear. A dog with ear mites may walk around with his head tilted, or may whine or yelp when he tries to scratch his ear. Check your dog's ears regularly for any unusual-looking substance.

If left untreated, ear mites are usually followed by a bacterial infection. This is very serious, and can lead to infection of the middle and inner ear, which can lead to an abscess in the brain, causing convulsions and death.

Ear mites are more commonly seen in puppies than adults. Ear mites are more common in dogs with long, hound-type ears than those with cropped or semi-upright ears. It's also more common in dogs who have long hair on their ears.

Other Medical Conditions

Dog Allergies

Allergies are caused by antigens, which in this case are also called allergens. An allergen is a substance that causes an allergic reaction. Some common allergens are pollen, mold spores, dust, foods and flea saliva. According to *Small Animal Allergy: A Practical Guide*, approximately 15 percent of American dogs suffer from allergies.

Some allergies occur from the allergen being carried through the air, as with pollen, mold spores, and dust. Others come from being eaten or bitten. Allergies can appear at any age, but usually they are detected within the first two years of a dog's life. If a dog is allergic to a substance the reaction will take place almost immediately.

When it comes to allergies, dogs are not like people. They don't get runny noses and sneeze a lot. It is more common for a dog to show symptoms involving the skin.

If your dog goes untreated, the itchy skin will lead to rubbing, licking and chewing the affected area. This can result in extensive and severe damage to the skin and lead to a bacterial infection. A dog scratching himself silly may seem like a minor issue to all but the tormented dog. But itching is the number one skin problem seen by veterinarians.

Let's take a look at some of the common allergens. Pollen is a well-known allergen to people. Dogs also suffer from pollen allergies, with ragweed and grasses being the most common. Mold spores are microscopic particles that produce the mildew smell, common to damp dark places like your basement. Spores are carried on the air currents. Mold spores are potent allergens to both dogs and people. House dust is a combination of fine particulate matter that floats in the air. Dander is dead skin that flakes off. It's a common allergen. Feathers and food are also common causes of allergic reactions.

The best prevention is to avoid the allergy-causing substance. Sometimes this is not always possible with the airborne allergens.

If, however, the allergy is caused by food, you can avoid it, providing you know what caused the reaction in the first place.

A veterinarian can make an evaluation using a skin test and his knowledge of the history and background of the dog's symptoms. Depending on the diagnosis, your veterinarian may prescribe antihistamine or corticosteroid treatments to help relieve the dog's symptoms, or may have you change the dog's diet if he suspects a food allergy.

Fleabite Allergic Dermatitis

Fleabite allergic dermatitis (FAD) is a major cause of skin problems in dogs. Some dog owners refer to this condition as summer itch. FAD is an allergic reaction to flea bites. This allergy is a hypersensitive reaction to the components of the fleas' saliva.

FAD can develop at any time during your dog's life, and it can appear very suddenly. Dermatitis is defined as an inflammation of the skin. Inflammation is the tissue's response to an injury and is characterized by pain, swelling, redness and heat.

Symptoms of FAD include intense itching. The skin will feel hot to your touch and will be red and swollen where the flea has bitten. Your dog will be constantly scratching and licking. A secondary bacterial infection may develop if the FAD goes untreated. The area affected by the fleas will become dry and crusty, the skin will become thickened and your dog will become bald in that spot.

The back and tail area, the areas most affected by fleas, are also the most affected by FAD. Effective treatment involves removing the fleas from the dogs and the environment (see page 147) as well as treating the secondary bacterial infection with antibiotics. Many veterinarians will place the dog on corticosteroids to relieve the itch. These may be good for the short term; however, the long-term cure involves aggressively eliminating the fleas from the environment.

Long-term use of corticosteroids may not be good for your dog. There are several other products on the market that may help to relieve the itch without using corticosteroids. Many veterinarians recommend the use of antihistamines or fatty acid supplements. There are also sprays and shampoos that may alleviate the urge to scratch.

Antiseptics Versus Disinfectants

To wrap up our section on preventive health, lets look at the difference between antiseptics and disinfectants. Both kill or prevent the growth of microorganisms.

Antiseptics are for use on living animals and won't hurt the host. Disinfectants are for inanimate objects, killing everything in sight.

The ideal disinfectant is stable—it won't lose effectiveness in light or air. Hydrogen peroxide, for example, always comes in a brown bottle because it loses its usefulness when exposed to light. The ideal disinfectant won't lose its power upon contact with organic materials, readily dissolves in water and is biodegradable. Properly diluted, it will kill many forms of microorganisms, yet have minimal effects on man or animals. A good disinfectant will be noncorrosive and have a minimal amount of offensive odor.

Now that we know the ideal, let's examine the most commonly used disinfectants:

The most commonly used kennel disinfectant is household chlorine bleach, mixed one part bleach with thirty parts water. It's cheap, readily available, and easy to use.

Bleach's effectiveness is vastly reduced in the presence of organic material, meaning it may not kill all of the microbes in feces, food, blood and vomit because it's busy oxidizing the organic material rather than the microbes.

Chlorine bleach, iodine and hydrogen peroxide should never be used on uncoated metal crates or chain link fences. They are oxidizing agents and you'll get a good case of rust.

Iodine is a good antiseptic and may be used to soak high-quality stainless steel grooming instruments between their use on successive animals. Iodophors, like Betadine, are less toxic than tincture of iodine, yet have the same killing power.

Hydrogen peroxide is good for washing and cleansing wounds but is a poor antiseptic. Neither iodine nor peroxide is a great disinfectant.

Alcohol can be used as an antiseptic and as a disinfectant. The key has to do with the concentration of the alcohol. Isopropyl alcohol in a 70 percent concentration is much more effective than 90 percent alcohol, which evaporates faster than it can work. Alcohol is a better antiseptic than a disinfectant.

Hospitals and labs use products that are close to ideal. They are O-Syl®, Amphyl® spray and Roccal®.

O-Syl® is a biodegradable disinfectant-detergent made for use in hospitals, institutions and industrial facilities. When it comes to disinfecting, this is the real thing.

It kills bacteria, including staph, tuberculosis, and pseudomonas, and viruses, such as herpes simplex, vaccinia, influenza and adenovirus type 2. It also kills disease-causing fungi, as well as preventing the growth of mold and mildew.

O-Syl® works in hard water and in the presence of organic matter. The disinfectant is good (which is why hospitals use it), but unfortunately, it's corrosive, and in concentrated form can cause eye and skin irritation as well as a variety of internal problems.

Like any cleaning product, keep it well away from children and pets. When you are cleaning, remove them from the area until you are completely finished and the cleaning materials have been put away. Follow label instructions completely, and wear safety equipment such as rubber gloves. Avoid contact with animal or human skin.

These products are available at some janitorial supply companies.

Products such as ProZema® Animal Quarters Disinfectant are an all-in-one disinfectant, detergent and deodorant capable of killing parvovirus, bacteria and herpes simplex. Look for products such as this at kennel or grooming supply houses.

11

First Aid

Do you know what to do if your dog is hit by a car? Do you know what plants are poisonous to your dog? Do you know when to call a veterinarian?

First aid is temporary emergency care for the injured dog. However, it is not a substitute for proper veterinary care. Improperly treating a dog can be more devastating than the injury itself. Use this section as a guideline for handling health crises, but once the animal has been stabilized, get in touch with a veterinarian immediately.

Normal Vital Signs of a Dog

The dog's normal temperature ranges from 100.5 to 102.5 degrees Fahrenheit. A normal pulse will run between 70 and 160 heartbeats per minute (up to 180 in toy breeds or 220 in puppies). A femoral pulse can be felt on the inside of the dog's thigh. Normally, a dog will breathe ten to thirty times a minute.

General First-Aid Rules

Here are some basics of first aid for your dog:

Emergency Phone Numbers

Post your veterinarian's phone number on the phone, as well as the number of a veterinarian who handles twenty-four-hour emergencies. Get a veterinarian or an emergency veterinary service on the phone for advice and to arrange for the next step.

Muzzle

Use a muzzle to avoid getting bitten by a panicky dog. Do not muzzle the dog if his mouth is bleeding—unless it is absolutely necessary. In that case, leave the muzzle on only until the dog calms down or has arrived safely at the veterinarian's office.

Bleeding

Stop it fast. Apply steady pressure over the wound until the bleeding stops. This may take several minutes. Use whatever you have to help stop the bleeding: a shirt, a towel, or even just your hand. A pressure bandage works best.

Tourniquet

Don't use a tourniquet unless it is absolutely necessary. Talk to a veterinarian before applying one.

Broken Limbs

Splint a broken limb. Even if you only suspect that the leg is broken, you should go ahead and make a splint to immobilize it. A splint can be made from anything that will stiffly hold the limb in position and keep it from moving. Use anything that works, such as a stick, wooden board, towel, rolled-up newspaper or magazine. Tie the splint with a sock, nylon or gauze. Avoid moving the broken limb out of position. Once the splint is applied, seek veterinary care.

Deep Wounds

Keep all wounds clean, but don't try to clean a deep wound. The veterinarian will clean the wound before suturing.

Paralysis

Do not lift a dog who seems paralyzed. Paralysis indicates a possible spinal cord injury. Always use a stiff board to support the animal when moving. Gently slide the board under the dog, then lift the board with the dog on it.

Big Dog

Don't carry a big dog in your arms. It is harder for your dog to breathe and could make injuries more serious. Use an improvised stretcher.

Small Dog

It is fine to carry a smaller dog in your arms. Hold it so that you give balanced support to each leg.

Medication

Give medication only on the advice of a veterinarian. Some medications work fine for people, but not for animals. Nonaspirin pain relievers, for example, can be lethal to dogs.

When Your Dog Needs to See a Veterinarian

In my many years of working with every imaginable animal— from aardvarks to zebras—I've found that prompt attention to health concerns is essential. Minor problems can turn into major problems if left untreated. That's why it's important to seek professional medical advice if you are at all unsure about the extent of a problem or how to treat it. In the long run, this course of action usually saves money, and may save your pet's life.

Those of us trained in zoology also know the important role that being observant can play. Getting a sense of what normal, healthy behavior is for the animal—through regular observation and daily examination—is important. We are the bridge to successful communications between pet and veterinarian. When there is a problem, the detailed behavioral information we provide often serves as a basis for the diagnosis the veterinarian makes.

JOAN EMBERY

~

Here are some important symptoms to watch for. If your dog has any of them, take your dog to a veterinarian.

* Drinking excessive amounts of water
* Frequent urination
* Straining during urination
* Difficulty defecating
* Persistent diarrhea
* Persistent vomiting
* Lumps beneath the skin
* Persistent cough
* Abnormal teeth or gums, extremely bad breath
* Loss of appetite and weight loss
* Hair loss—more than normal shedding—bald spots
* Abnormal look to the eyes, especially in older animals
* Pawing at ears, shaking head
* Any unusual discharge
* Any hard-to-explain change in behavior
* Uncontrollable bleeding
* Extreme difficulty in breathing

• Convulsions
• Unconsciousness
• Shock
• Sudden paralysis

Signs of Poisoning

• Dilated or pinpoint pupils, eyes watering
• Weak breathing, difficult breathing, respiratory spasms
• Severe pain, slobbering, vomiting and perhaps bloody diarrhea
• Cold body, fast heartbeat
• Twitching, staggering, unusual excitability
• Rear-end paralysis
• Coma

Household Poisons

Although we briefly discussed poisoning in the "Puppy-Proofing Your Home" section (pp 25–28), it is important to remember that many older dogs may become exposed to some common household poisons. For example, many reported poisonings involve ethylene glycol, which is the active ingredient in antifreeze. Other potential sources of problems include rat poisons, insecticides, insect repellents (DEET), boric acid and drugs. A dog will often come in contact with lawn fertilizers, which may cause local irritation and/or systemic signs (vomiting, diarrhea). Be sure to follow the manufacturer's or lawn care specialist's directions. Even a common penny, if ingested, can lead to zinc poisoning! If you are concerned that your dog has been exposed to a poison, contact your veterinarian immediately. Another invaluable source of information is the Illinois Animal Poison Information Center at 1-900-660-0000. This call costs $2.95 a minute.

Diagnosis of Plant Poisoning

The diagnosis of plant poisoning in dogs is not an easy or precise procedure. Any case of sudden death or illness with no apparent cause is commonly considered to be a poisoning. However, this may not always be correct.

Generally, no set of symptoms provides all the information necessary to make an irrefutable diagnosis of plant poisoning. Keeping a descriptive list of all the plants in your house and yard can help to track down the culprit in cases of mysterious illness.

Additional information essential to a poisonous plant diagnosis includes such things as identification of the plants available to the dog, approximate time from ingesting the plant to appearance of symptoms and the type of symptoms.

Poison Prevention Is Easier Than Treatment

Successfully treating a poisoned dog is much more difficult than successfully preventing a poisoning by plants. Since diagnosis is so tough, it usually cannot be made before the dog dies.

Here are some other suggestions to prevent plant poisonings. First, don't plant bulbs while the puppy or dog is playing in the yard. Many bulbs are lethal. They're shaped like little balls and are great to play with. Then, too, many dogs think that what Mom or Dad buries is fair game for them to dig up.

Take notice if your dog is digging under your favorite azalea bush and then suddenly becomes ill. Azaleas can sicken your dog.

When hanging the mistletoe, place it in a plastic bag so the toxic berries can't drop to the floor. Better yet, buy the plastic variety and the berries won't fall off. Mistletoe berries can kill your dog.

Learn the poisonous plants common to your area. Know the symptoms that generally indicate plant poisoning for the plants you have in your house or yard.

Some Common Poisonous Plants

How do you find out which of your plants are poisonous? Your local poison control center can provide you with a list of poisonous plants found in your area. The following list of poisonous plants, while not complete, will give you some idea of the common, yet deadly, plants lurking about your house. If your pet eats these plants—or parts of them such as leaves, stems, roots, berries or beans—he can get sick. Again, the symptoms may include digestive upset, depression, disorientation, breathing difficulty, nervous excitement, coma or death. Keep animals away from them!

If you suspect your dog has eaten any of these plants, call a veterinarian immediately. Your local poison control center can also be a helpful emergency resource for animal poisonings.

Plants with poisonous leaves include bleeding heart, Dutchman's-breeches, foxglove, poinsettia, yew, rhubarb and elderberry. Elderberry berries, however, are safe. Unsafe berries include those of the yew and mistletoe.

Poisonous bulbs include hyacinth, narcissus and daffodil. Also watch out for both the leaves and flowers of the azalea, oleander leaves and branches, the below-ground stems of the iris, the castor bean, larkspur seeds and seedlings and golden chain seed pods.

Other poisonous plants are the autumn crocus, rhododendron, lily of the valley, oak (in the spring), water hemlock, chokecherry, lupine and milkweed.

(Note: This is only a partial list of poisonous plants.)

Restraint: The Emergency Muzzle

Here's how to make a quick emergency muzzle from nylons or other handy material.

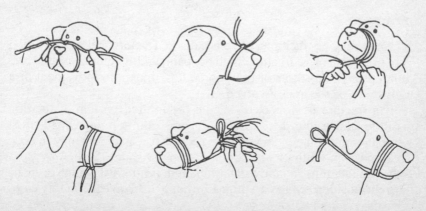

First, tie a loose knot in the middle of the material, making a large loop. Slip the loop over your dog's nose, sliding it behind the soft spot of the nose, about midway between the dog's eyes and the tip of his nose.

Quickly tighten the loop over the nose, then bring the ends under the chin and tie again. Pass the ends of the material under the ears and tie behind the head.

For a short-faced bulldog-type nose, add an additional step. Take the ends of the material from behind his head and bring them forward to the nose loop. Slip the material under the loop and take it back around. Then tie it off behind the head. This will prevent the muzzle from slipping off his nose.

Transporting an Injured Dog

After a dog has been injured, it will usually lie or sit in the most comfortable position it can find. Try not to change the dog's position, yet move the animal in a manner that will not aggravate the injured area. If you suspect spinal injuries, try to keep him as flat as possible. Slide a board under the dog to pick him up yet also prevent movement of the spine. Please remember that injured dogs are often frightened and/or apprehensive. Use care when moving animals. Apply a muzzle if necessary.

Specific Injuries and How to Handle Them

Fracture

Any break or crack in a bone is called a fracture. Signs indicating the presence of a fracture include pain and swelling around the injured area, lameness of the injured leg, unnatural movement or a deformity of the area involved.

If a fracture is suspected, handle the injured portion of the dog as little as possible. Most dogs suffering from a fracture will resist your attempts to help, so you may need to use an emergency muzzle to avoid being bitten.

Never attempt to move the fractured limb. Just splint it in its current position. Make a splint from any stiff object such as cardboard or rolled-up newspapers. Follow the pattern of the injured limb. If the limb is at a ninety-degree angle, splint it that way. Make sure the splint gives the limb plenty of support.

If you suspect a spinal column injury, call a veterinarian for advice before you attempt to move the dog. If the dog is in the middle of traffic, do your best to place it on a board of some sort. Incorrectly moving a dog with a spinal injury can result in paralysis.

Shock

Shock is a condition in which the circulatory system stops functioning properly. The dog does not get enough oxygen from the bloodstream, and wastes build up within the body. Shock can be brought about by a number of causes, including fractures, blood loss and sudden injury.

What an Animal in Shock Looks Like

An animal in shock will have a glassy-eyed appearance. He will be taking quick short breaths and have a rapid but weak pulse and a low body temperature. A sure sign of shock is a slow capillary refill time. Check for this by pressing your finger firmly against the animal's gum until it turns white. Then remove your finger and note how long it takes for the pink color to return. Normal is one to two seconds for a dog. A longer time indicates shock.

What to Do for an Animal in Shock

Treatment for an animal in shock is the same as for a person in shock. Keep the dog warm, covering him with a towel or a blanket. A dog in shock loses body heat and should be kept warm, but not hot.

Slightly lower the dog's head in relation to the rest of his body. This helps increase the flow of blood to his brain and will help prevent any possible brain damage. Get the dog immediately to a veterinarian!

Hemorrhage—Severe Bleeding

Severe bleeding can lead to shock and death. A hemorrhage is severe bleeding, either internally or externally.

Blood loss may occur from a visible wound or it can occur internally with the blood pooling within the tissue. Bleeding from an open wound is obvious, while internal bleeding may not be discovered until the animal goes into shock.

Any time the dog has suffered a physical injury he should be checked by a veterinarian for possible internal bleeding or damage.

Burns

Burns vary in the degree of severity. They should always be checked by a veterinarian so the extent of tissue damage may be determined. Burns are extremely susceptible to infection and should never be touched until you have thoroughly washed your hands. It's important that the burned area be touched only by sterile or clean material. Burns also get wet and sticky, so never cover a burned area with any material that will stick to the damaged area. Do not put butter on a burn. That only worsens the problem.

Since burns can be caused by an electrical source, be sure the electricity is off before you touch your dog—or you could be shocked and burned also.

Foreign Objects

Dogs, like children, sometimes seem to be magnets for foreign objects. Whether a foreign object should be removed by you will depend on the object. If a dog has an object embedded in his skin and it would obviously cause more damage to remove it, get him to the veterinarian.

Treat all eye injuries with extreme care. Prevent the dog from irritating it further while you are in route to the veterinary hospital.

Check your dog for burrs every time he's been out romping in the weeds. Be sure to check under his tail, between his toes and in his ears.

Here are some more common items that may be tempting to your dog. Keep them out of the dog's reach, as your dog may not survive a meal of these items. Dogs will get into trouble with fishhooks, knives, razor blades, needles, pins, chicken bones, wood, aluminum foil, TV dinner trays, balloons, office supplies such as staples or paper clips, pin cushions and other sewing supplies and any other objects a dog might think about eating.

Heat Stroke

Heat stroke is a condition characterized by the dog's high body temperature of 105 to 110 degrees Fahrenheit. A body temperature this high can cause permanent brain damage and death.

The dog's owner is almost always the cause of heat stroke. Some owners leave their dogs unattended in parked cars in warm weather. Others leave their dogs outside without any shade or water. These people are irresponsible, putting their dogs in danger of death from heat stroke. High humidity, hot weather, lack of shade and being in a hot car (even with the windows open) can all contribute to the occurrence of heat stroke.

Aside from high body temperature, other signs of heat stroke include heavy panting or rapid, difficult breathing while sitting still or lying on his side. If you try to get your dog to walk, he will stumble or collapse in a heap.

What to Do if Heat Stroke Occurs

If you think your dog has heat stroke, act immediately to cool him. Cooling is most effective where the most blood flows. Concentrate your first efforts on the main arteries on either side of the throat which supply the brain, the belly area where the blood flows to the organs and the groin where the blood flows to and from the legs. Be sure to cool the skin, not just the fur.

Act quickly and use whatever you have at hand. Immerse the dog in a tub of cold water. Place ice packs on either side of the throat, belly and groin. Make a U-shaped ice-pack collar to cool the arteries alongside the throat. Spray the entire body with cold water from a hose. Do anything else you can think of to cool him down immediately, such as putting your dog in a pool or stream while holding his head up so he can breathe. Use ice from an ice cooler or even a cold drink or wrap wet towels around the neck and chest. Fast cooling of the blood and body are the keys to ending heat stroke. How you do it isn't important.

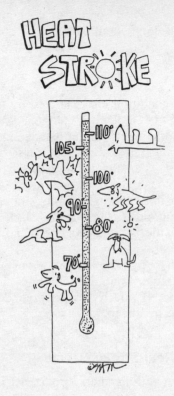

After the dog's breathing has returned to normal, get him to the nearest veterinary hospital, as the symptoms may reappear.

Prevention of Heat Stroke

Heat stroke is preventable with a little common sense. Never leave your dog in a car on a warm day. When it is 75 degrees Fahrenheit outside, the temperature inside the car will reach 102 degrees in ten minutes and 120 degrees in thirty minutes—even with the windows open! Your dog cannot tolerate these temperatures and has no way of cooling himself. He'll die if you leave him unattended.

Always provide outdoor dogs with adequate shade and water. Bring ice water with you when you and your dog travel. Avoid heavy exercise when the temperature is above 80 degrees.

12

Traveling with Your Dog

Taking Your Dog on the Family Vacation

THE FIRST PLACE YOU AND YOUR DOG MUST TRAVEL TO BEFORE YOU embark on a journey together is the veterinarian's office. Inform your veterinarian that you and your dog are going to go on a vacation together and ask if there is any medication for motion sickness you should have on hand or any other items you should take with you. Many states require a dog have a health certificate showing that he has had his vaccinations and that he is in good health. You should obtain this health certificate a day or so before your departure date.

Lodging Arrangements for You and Your Dog

Plan in advance; find out what the rules and regulations are regarding dogs for each hotel you wish to stay at. Not all hotels will accept pets. Disney World in Florida has special accommodations for pets. You can drop your dog off at their beautiful kennel facilities in the morning and pick him up on the way out. There is no charge except for a deposit on the key that is refunded upon its return. Yosemite National Park hotel and camping area does not allow dogs. However, a kennel is operated during the tourist season to accommodate your pet. Many places provide facilities for your pet. Call the hotel or vacation area to find out what the rules are regarding pets.

Things to Bring with You

1. Bring the dog's crate or his bed. It is also a good idea to pack an old sheet or bedspread to place on the hotel's bed so the hotel won't complain about dog hairs or his muddy or sandy feet when he jumps on the bed. Of course we all know that dogs aren't supposed to be on the hotel furniture.

2. Pack a small suitcase for your dog and include his water and food bowls, his grooming items and his play toys.

3. Include paper towels and dishwashing soap to clean his food and water bowl.

4. Pack plenty of trash bags, a pooper scoop, or baggies for picking up your dog's droppings.

5. Pack some bath towels should your dog get caught in the rain. Hotel towels are for people, not dogs, and hotels frown upon their towels being used for wiping dogs' feet or the like.

6. As a precautionary measure to guard against stomach upset or diarrhea for the first few days, bring a gallon jug of your dog's drinking water with you from home.

7. Pack your dog's collar and a twenty-foot leash so he can do some exploring and running with you.

8. Pack a first-aid kit for your dog. Kits are commercially available from most pet stores. Make sure you have supplies to remove ticks if you are going to be in an area where they live.

9. If you are going to be in an area where the sun is shining and the weather is hot, bring a tarp or some type of portable shade for your dog. Heat is your dog's worst enemy on the road. *Never leave your dog in a car, even with the window down. Always try to park in a shady area.*

Feeding Your Dog on the Road

Do not feed your dog or give him water for at least two hours before your departure, especially if he is prone to motion sickness. Make sure you give your dog plenty of time to relieve himself before you leave.

Do not decide to change his diet before you go on vacation. A sudden change in diet can cause some digestive upset. If you do want to change your dog's diet, do it at least two weeks before you leave or wait until you return from your trip. Take your dog's current diet with you. If you are using a brand that is available nationally, take enough for the first few days. If you are feeding a brand that is not nationally distributed, then take enough for the entire trip.

Car Travel Tips

1. It is always best to travel with your dog safe and secure in his crate.

2. However, if your dog isn't crate-trained don't allow him to sit in the front seat. He could inadvertently interfere with your driving.

3. *Never allow your dog to ride in the back of a car or truck unrestrained.* Safety restraints are available for attaching to the seat belts inside the car or truck. Many states are now passing laws requiring dogs to be restrained by a safety harness when riding in the back of trucks. If you intend to have your dog travel in the back of your truck, make sure he has shade and a place to lie down. If you are going to place his crate in the back, make sure the crate is secured and that your dog is safe from the elements and a possible change in the weather.

4. Never allow your dog to travel with his head sticking out the window. The dog could be injured from small stones or other objects kicked up by moving traffic.

5. Never allow your dog to run loose at rest areas. Keep your pet on a leash and confined to the "pets only" area. Most rest stops have restricted areas where dogs are not welcome. Obey the rules.

Car Sickness and How to Prevent It

Some dogs suffer from car sickness because of the motion itself; others become car sick because they are nervous and uncomfortable about riding in the car. If the dog is comfortable and relaxed when riding in the car but still gets sick, see your veterinarian for motion sickness pills for your dog. If your dog is the nervous type, here are some suggestions that might help.

1. The best way to head off the problem is to teach your dog when he is a puppy. The first thing to do is to get the dog used to just being in the car while it is parked. Place him in his traveling crate or on the back seat, praise him, feed him a treat or two and make him feel relaxed about the situation. You can bring his dinner out to the car and feed him there as well. The idea is to make the dog as comfortable in the car as he is in the house. Whatever you did to make the dog comfortable in the house is the same procedure you will do here.

2. After you have practiced this for awhile and the dog seems comfortable, start the motor, but keep the car stationary. Pay attention to your dog's reaction. If he seems nervous do not turn the engine off; instead turn the radio on to some soft music station. Encourage the dog to play with you. After he has attempted to play with you, turn the motor and the radio off. If you turn the motor off at the minute the dog becomes upset, you may reinforce the behavior of becoming upset. Slowly increase the time the motor is running. This is a gradual process, during which you should continue to monitor your dog's reaction. Once he seems comfortable with the motor running for about three minutes, see if he'll eat his dinner out there. Praise the dog after the motor has been turned off and you are out of the car.

3. After the dog is comfortable and relaxed, put him in the car and back down the driveway, stop for a few seconds and drive back up the driveway. Praise the dog and go for a walk. Each day increase the distance you drive the car. Once your dog

can handle going around the block, take him to a park to have some fun.

4. Don't feed the dog at least two hours before you embark on your first long trip. Feed him upon your arrival or return when he is relaxed.

Air Travel

As you can imagine, since I frequently fly with animals of all types, I am very familiar with the challenges and potential pitfalls of air travel. One of the more challenging flying animal experiences I ever had involved getting a boa constrictor from San Diego to Wichita for a press conference. The snake missed its Denver connection and was returned to San Diego. Back in San Diego, all the airline staff knew was that the snake had to get to Wichita, so they shipped it back to Denver. By then it had missed the last flight out and was shipped out the next morning. It finally made it to Wichita at the last possible minute and got to the press conference just in the nick of time. I always say that it is the only snake that became a frequent flier— literally—overnight!

JOAN EMBERY

~

Traveling by air with a pet, like any other kind of travel, requires preparation. There are three things you will need, regardless of the type of air travel you choose:

1. A sturdy crate that is properly sized, provides adequate ventilation and is clearly labeled "This End Up," "Live Animals." Include your name and a telephone number and the pet's destination.

2. A recent health certificate from your veterinarian to prove that your pet is up to date on all vaccinations and is generally healthy.

3. Reservations! Call ahead. Although this may seem obvious, many people don't realize that even in the cargo hold of a passenger plane, space is limited. Also ask for specific rules and regulations including feeding and water provisions.

There are also three different types of air travel for pets:

1. In the cabin, on some airlines, is allowed if the pet's crate fits under the seat in front of you.
2. In the cargo hold of a passenger plane—the same plane you are on—the pet goes as baggage.
3. Air Freight on a passenger plane—a useful option if you need to send your pet somewhere you are not going.

Here are some general guidelines that can help you to prepare for a safe and comfortable flight for your pet. However, because rules, regulations and costs vary from airline to airline, and some airlines don't even accept animals, we strongly recommend that you check with the airline you plan to use several weeks before your trip. They will be able to provide you with the specific information you need to ensure that they will be able to transport your pet, and that you will be able to comply with their requirements.

Cost

When your pet flies with you, either in the passenger or baggage section of the plane you are on, the cost varies from airline to airline, so check with the airline you plan to use. One of the least expensive options, which only works with smaller pets, is going the in-cabin route, where the animal flies in its crate under your seat. However, reservations must be made well in advance of the trip.

Airline charges are structured by the size and weight of your animal in its crate.

In some cities, there are kennels which will take your pet and schedule the flight reservations, buy the proper size crate and put your pet on the airline for you. For example, in Los Angeles, there is a company called Vet Pet that performs this service.

Safety

The primary safety consideration for a pet traveling on an airplane is heatstroke due to delays and excessive outside temperatures. It is very important to ensure that the outside temperature does not exceed 85° F or drop below 45° F for up to four consecutive hours. Booking a *direct* early morning or late evening flight can help avoid excessive temperatures. Airline regulations determine when and where your dog can be transported.

If there is even a possibility of a temperature problem, it is your responsibility to verify that the necessary precautions for the entire route including temperature, delays and connecting flights have been taken. The airline is not trying to make your life difficult, but rather to protect the health of your pet.

For more information on transporting your dog, a fact sheet called "Transportation Tips" is available from the Animal and Plant Inspection Service by sending a self-addressed, stamped envelope to APHIS, LPA/PI, 6505 Belcrest Road, Room 613, Hyattsville, MD 20782. The AKC is also a good source of information on international transport of purebreeds.

Timing

When sending your pet on an airplane, you will need to plan to arrive at the airport *much earlier* than you normally would because there is paperwork to fill out. If you send your pet via air freight, their offices are generally in a totally separate area than the passenger terminals. Make sure to write "live animals" in over 1" letters on all sides of the crate with arrows showing the upright position.

Another factor that involves timing, as any traveler can tell you, is making connections. When your pet is traveling in the baggage section, and you both need to make a connecting flight, *you always need to make sure that your pet's crate gets loaded onto the next flight*. The crew on the first flight and the desk personnel for the connecting flight usually can check this for you—and you should ask both to do so. You should alert these personnel to the situation as soon as possible, particularly if the first flight is delayed for any length of time.

Be a Considerate, Responsible Dog Owner

Dogs will continue to be allowed at hotels only if their owners are considerate and act responsibly.

1. Keep your pet under supervision at all times.
2. Keep him leashed.
3. Do not allow him to wander and disturb the other hotel guests.
4. Never leave your dog loose in a hotel room. He should be crated when left alone.
5. Walk your dog as far away as possible from lawns, flower beds and public areas. Keep baggies in your pocket to pick up after your dog.
6. Never take him into a dining room, lobby, lounge area or pool area.
7. You should not allow your dog to jump on the hotel furniture.
8. If your dog does cause any damage, volunteer to pay the costs.
9. Remember, responsible dog owners obey all the rules and regulations regarding their pets. They are courteous and considerate to all hotel guests and employees.

13

Dog Shows

Understanding the Dog Show

Dog shows are fun—if you know what you're looking at. At first, it can seem quite bewildering. Dogs of every variety are moving, waiting and barking. The basics, though, aren't difficult, and you'll probably be hooked in no time.

Dog shows exist to give owners a place to compete their dog against similar dogs. Winners, as the best representatives of their breed, are used in selective breeding programs to improve the quality of the breed. So dog shows are really a tool used to help improve the dog's breed.

Most dog shows follow the very detailed rules of the American Kennel Club, which governs nearly all of the activities involving purebred dogs in the United States. The United Kennel Club also sanctions various shows, primarily for breeds not recognized by the AKC. Most other countries also have their own kennel clubs to handle these same functions.

The AKC currently recognizes 138 breeds, broken down into seven groups plus a Miscellaneous Class for breeds that aren't now recognized by the AKC but are seeking recognition. Miscellaneous Class dogs can't win points or compete in group judging.

Dog shows start with many contestants, eliminating those of lesser quality in subsequent rounds until only the best of the best remain. The ultimate winner is titled Best in Show. Even at the lower levels, the competition is important, with the winners receiving ribbons, championship points, Best of Breed and Group Winner honors.

There are three types of dog shows: All-Breed Conformation, Specialty Conformation, and Obedience. They are often held at the same time under the sponsorship of one club.

In the conformation show, many breeds of dog participate. Each breed is judged according to its own breed standard—an authorized, written description of what makes the perfect dog of that breed. Judges are trained and well-practiced in identifying the good and bad points for each breed, based on the breed standard.

Specialty shows are dog shows for just one breed. The rules are the same as at an all-breed show except there is no Group or Best in Show competition—only Best of Breed. Points toward a dog's becoming a Champion are awarded at AKC-recognized all-breed and specialty conformation shows.

The catalog for a show is the official program. It lists the dogs, their owners, their handlers, breeders, classes and points to be awarded, plus where and when the judging will happen. You can usually buy the catalog near the admission gate.

Some shows are "benched." These shows have an area where dogs are kept on low benches when they're not being judged. You can walk by them and look (they are arranged by breed), but the general rule is not to touch a dog without permission of the owner. Some dogs get nervous around people; others have just undergone hours of grooming to make them look their best.

Show Grooming

Every dog show has an area for grooming. You can watch this amazing process as the dog is transformed into an absolutely perfect creature. Appearance counts for a great deal in the show ring, so grooming is an important part of the process. Again, don't touch without permission. Remember, the people doing the grooming are seriously involved with making their dog look like a winner, so it's not usually the best time to engage them in conversation.

The Judging

Each show ring has a number. The catalog will tell you the breeds and classes that will be judged in each ring and when.

Each breed is judged alone, with males and females in separate competition. There are six regular classes for each breed: Puppy (six to nine months), Puppy (nine to twelve months), Novice, Bred-by-Exhibitor, American-Bred, and Open. According to dog show regulations, a puppy becomes a grown dog when he's twelve months old. Puppy classes are usually entered for experience only.

The Novice Class is for puppies or dogs that have not won three first prizes in the Novice Class nor any points toward their championships.

The Bred-by-Exhibitor Class is for dogs who are shown by their breeders or a member of the immediate family. There are usually only a few entries in this class.

The American-Bred Class is for all dogs, except champions, that were born in the United States through a mating that took place in this country.

The Open Class is open to any member of a breed, regardless of age, that has not yet completed its championship. Open Class dogs are usually mature and may be close to earning their championships.

Some shows also offer a class for Junior Showmanship. This is open to children handlers between the ages of ten and seventeen who have not won a first place in any of the Novice divisions. In this category, it's the handler who is judged, not the dog. No championship points are given; but a first-place win entitles a boy or girl to move on to more advanced classes.

Not all classes are offered at every show. It all depends upon how many dogs enter. Consult your catalog for what is at the show.

HOW A DOG SHOW WORKS

BEST IN SHOW

The winners of each Group compete for Best In Show (BIS) – the one dog who receives the top honor at this dog show.

HOUND GROUP	WORKING GROUP	TERRIER GROUP
includes Bloodhound	includes Great Dane	includes Fox Terrier

SPORTING GROUP	NON-SPORTING GROUP	HERDING GROUP
includes Labrador Retriever	includes Dalmatian	includes German Shepherd

TOY GROUP	GROUP COMPETITION
includes Pekingese	The Best of Breed Winners from each breed in the Group compete against each other. The 4 best get ribbons, and the best of each Group compete for Best In Show.

BEST OF BREED
Second place: Best of Opposite Sex

Only dogs who are Champions can enter the Best of Breed competition. However, Winners Dog and Winners Bitch are "invited" to participate.

BEST OF WINNERS

The only male and female to receive points toward their Championships. Second place is Reserve Winners Dog and Reserve Winners Bitch.

WINNERS DOG   **WINNERS BITCH**

PUPPY	NOVICE	BRED BY EXHIBITOR	AMERICAN BRED	OPEN
6-9 months 9-12 months or all under 1 year	Dogs 12 months to 2 years who look immature	The dog was bred by the person showing it	The dog was bred and born in the U.S.A.	Mature dogs at least a year old

These classes of competition are offered for males (dogs) and females (bitches) of each breed. The Blue Ribbon winners of each class compete against each other for Winners Dog and Winners Bitch.

Order of Judging

The males (called dogs) of each breed are judged first, and four placements are awarded in each class.

When all six classes have been judged, the first-place winners are called back to compete among themselves. The judge selects a Winner and a Reserve Winner (runner-up). The Winner receives points for his victory; the Reserve Winner does not.

Now the females (called bitches) of the same breed come into the ring and, class by class, compete as the males did. They receive similar ribbons to the ones won by the males, and in the winner's case, they also receive championship points.

The catalog will tell you how many points the winners receive. Points are awarded based on the number of dogs entered in a particular breed: the more dogs, the more points. While every win is valuable, a win of three, four or five points is known as a "major." To finish (win a championship) a dog needs fifteen points won under at least three different judges. These must include two majors, each under a different judge. No more than five points can be won in a single show.

Best of Breed is next determined by showing the Winner Dog and the Winner Bitch against dogs and bitches of the same breed who are already champions. No championship points are given for this award, though it carries a great deal of prestige. If the judge's selection for Best of Breed happens to be a male, he then selects a bitch to be Best of Opposite Sex (or vice versa). If the Winner Dog or Winner Bitch isn't chosen as Best of Breed, the judge selects one of the two as Best of Winners.

Every breed at the show goes through this same process, resulting in a Best for each breed. The Best of each breed then competes against each other, in the Group competition. The different Groups are Terrier, Working, Sporting, Non-sporting, Hound, Herding and Toy. The winners from each Group compete against each other before a special judge for Best in Show.

For more information on conformance and obedience, contact the AKC Show Plans Department for show schedules or the AKC Library for rules and regulations, at 51 Madison Avenue, New York, New York 10010. For more information on UKC conformance and obedience, contact the UKC at 100 East Kilgore Road, Kalamazoo, Michigan 49001.

Obedience Trials

Obedience trials also follow AKC regulations and use AKC-approved judges. They are usually held at the same time and place as the Conformation Shows. The obedience trial demonstrates the usefulness of the purebred dog. Even more so, it is a fun sport where the dogs are "working" at specified tasks.

Quality of the dog in terms of conformation is unimportant for obedience work—how the dog thinks and is trained is what counts. In fact, several organizations now offer obedience trials and titles for mixed-breed dogs—as long as they have been spayed or neutered. For AKC Trials, the dogs must be purebred and over six months of age. Most have been through extensive obedience training classes.

There are three major levels of training. The average dog in the Novice classes has had at least a year of work and is following practical commands used in everyday living, but not under everyday conditions. The second level is Open, which is more difficult, and the highest level is the Utility Class.

Titles and Points

Through the Novice Class, dogs earn the Companion Dog (CD) title; in the Open Class, the Companion Dog Excellent (CDX) title, and in the Utility Class, the Utility Dog (UD) title.

The team (handler and dog) competes against a top score of two hundred to win these AKC obedience titles. To earn a title, a team must qualify in three trials under three different judges by receiving at least one hundred and seventy points out of a possible two hundred. In each exercise, they must receive more than half of the available points.

Dogs who have won their UD title may go on to compete for Championship points toward an obedience trial championship (OTCH) as set forth in the AKC Obedience Regulations. Any dog that has placed 1st or 2d in the Utility Class receives points toward its OTCH.

How Obedience Trials Are Judged

In an obedience exercise, the dog is given one command or signal and must follow that command acceptably. The final score is affected by a variety of minor points. These include the willingness, enjoyment and precision of the dog and the smoothness of the handler.

Every exercise includes the heel position. All end with the dog sitting in front of the handler and on command going to the heel position. This involves sitting next to and parallel to the handler's left leg without crowding.

Other exercises include heeling and the recall, where the dog must come when a signal is given. In the sit-stay the dog must sit and stay until released, and in the down-stay, he must lie down and stay on command.

Obedience Classes and Titles

Class (Level of Training)	Title	Required Exercise
Sub-Novice (with leash/ no points)	No Title	Stand for exam, heel, come, long sit, long down on leash
Novice	Companion Dog (CD)	All of the above off leash
Open	Excellent (CDX)	All of the above plus: Heel off lead, drop on recall, retrieve on the flat and over jumps
Utility	Utility Dog (UD) title - Obedient Trial Champion (OTCH) - Champion of Record - Field Champion	All of the above plus: Hand signals/no verbal commands, scent discrimination, directed retrieve, directed jumping, group long sit/ long down exam

The long down involves lying down and staying for several minutes while the handler leaves the dog. Retrieval and jumping are interesting exercises, but even more interesting are the directed retrieve and scent discrimination. In the directed retrieve, the dog must know which object the handler is sending him to get and then bring back that specific object. The dog may be sent to pick up the glove on the left, for example, as opposed to the one on the right. In the scent discrimination exercise, one retrieval dumbbell is given to the handler to hold so that his "scent" is on only one dumbbell, and the dog must pick that one out from the other dumbbells spread out before him. It's fun to watch the dogs working their noses!

14

A Concise History of Dogs . . . and People

How did the relationship between dogs and people develop? According to scientists, the answer can most likely be found in the similarities between early man and the wolf . . . in everything from living habitat to survival techniques. All of today's 350+ breeds of dogs descended from wolves, a species that evolved in many of the same locations as early man.

Although we don't know exactly how wolves became dogs, archaeologists have put many pieces of this puzzle together. The clues they have unearthed enable us to make some educated guesses about when the wolf-like predecessors of the dog became part of man's family.

Common Ground

Around 30,000 years ago, during the end of the Pleistocene period, people hunted in groups and lived in small, tightly knit clans near the animals that were their food supply. By working as a team, people were able to successfully hunt large game, and one kill would feed everyone for a while. In this primitive society, adults hunted and adolescents stayed behind to tend to younger children and gather grains, nuts and berries for the group.

Like the people of that time, wolves were also social hunters that teamed up to kill large animals. They took care of their young, who stayed "home" in the den. Extremely intelligent, wolves had developed a social hierarchy, with the dominant male and female serving as leaders of the pack. They communicated with eye contact, facial expressions and body language. Wolves, too, lived near their prey—the same herds of animals hunted by humans.

Wolves ate the same food as our ancestors did, lived in social "packs" similar to human clans and, like people, communicated among themselves. Both species were skilled hunters, competing for the same game. Both were opportunistic feeders, finding food wherever and whenever they could. In fact, the earliest form of cooperation between these species may have occurred when wolves waited for the scraps from human kills with other scavengers. Some historians theorize that the promise of this food source may have led wolf packs to follow behind migratory human clans.

Thus, it seems wolves and people were in many ways a match for each other and it was only a matter of time before the two species joined forces.

Taming the Wolf

How were wolves first domesticated? What were the first steps in the process that ultimately led to dogs unique status as "man's best friend"? Over the centuries, scientists have developed a number of theories.

The first wolves to find their way into human society were probably orphaned pups. Based on explorers' interactions with American Indians, we know it was not uncommon for aboriginal women to nurse orphaned bear cubs, monkeys or puppies along with their own babies. These animals often became pets, fawned over like a favorite child. It was in this way that domestication of the wolf probably began.

Charles Darwin's cousin, Francis Galton, a nineteenth-century scientist, theorized that domestication was both the result of "a vast number of half-unconscious attempts" and the fact that domestic animals must have "been found useful to early man." Useful as a source of companionship—and a food source when tribes had poor hunting seasons.

Around 9,000 years ago, hunter-gatherers in western Asia began to keep herds of animals such as sheep and goats, which provided a more stable and convenient food source than hunting game. People also began to grow their own grains, another food that could be stored. This enabled a shift from a largely migratory way of life into a more sedentary, agricultural mode. This major change for humanity also led to new kinds of interactions between man and dogs, who were trained to help maintain the flocks and protect human settlements.

Physical Evolution: From Wolf to Dog

Domestication does some interesting things to an animal. The differences between wolves and dogs are a good example of the effects of domestication on many species. Animals removed from their mother and her environment, and raised in captivity from an early age, may exhibit changes, both behavioral and even physical, compared to their wild siblings. The body is more plastic and changeable than might be thought and because of changes in diet, activity and other factors, minor physical differences may be noticed. These differences may be mediated by changes in hormone levels.

Within several generations, the body size of domesticated animals becomes smaller than those of its wild counterparts. This change is most pronounced in the face and jaw, which shorten. As a result, the teeth get crowded together and eventually they also become smaller. The anatomy of today's dog bears this out. The dog has a shorter snout, a smaller jaw, and teeth that are both smaller and more crowded together than that of the wolf.

These clues enable archaeologists to tell whether or not they have found the bones of a domesticated animal. The earliest remains of a domesticated dog ever found (to date) were excavated at Jaguar

EVOLUTION OF

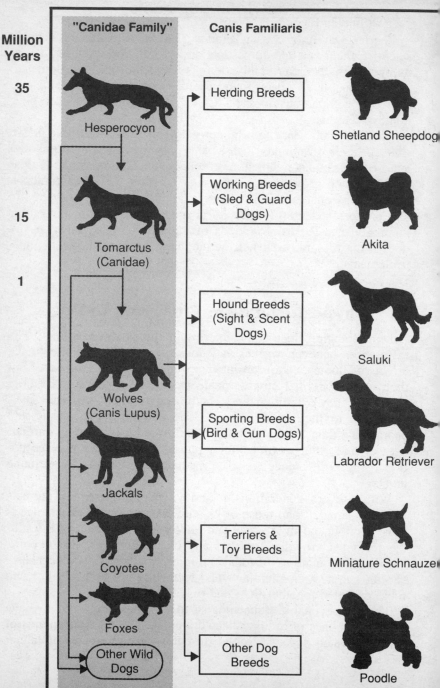

Million Years	"Canidae Family"	Canis Familiaris	
35	Hesperocyon	Herding Breeds	Shetland Sheepdog
15	Tomarctus (Canidae)	Working Breeds (Sled & Guard Dogs)	Akita
1	Wolves (Canis Lupus)	Hound Breeds (Sight & Scent Dogs)	Saluki
	Jackals	Sporting Breeds (Bird & Gun Dogs)	Labrador Retriever
	Coyotes	Terriers & Toy Breeds	Miniature Schnauzer
	Foxes		
	Other Wild Dogs	Other Dog Breeds	Poodle

DOMESTIC DOGS

——— Popular Breeds ———

German Shepherd   Collie   Briard   Pembroke Welsh Corgi

Siberian Husky   Rottweiler   Boxer   Doberman Pinscher

Greyhound   Irish Wolfhound   Beagle   Dachshund

Cocker Spaniel   Golden Retriever   English Springer Spaniel   Irish Setter

Yorkshire Terrier   Shih Tzu   Pomeranian   Chihuahua

Chow Chow   Dalmatian   Lhasa Apso   Bulldog

Cave, Idaho. Fossil fragments from its jawbone were judged to be nearly 12,000 years old, and archaeologists believe the dog lived sometime between 9500 and 8400 B.C. The dog was probably similar in size and form to Eskimo dogs.

Domesticated animals who are well fed will have a layer of fat under the skin. In the wild, animals tend to collect fat around the internal organs. Animals kept by people will have a smaller brain mass relative to their body size, and smaller sense organs. Estrous, or heat, cycles differ, too. Dogs in the wild come into heat just once a year; domesticated dogs come into season twice a year.

The Development of Breeds

As these changes took place, wolf/dogs were also developing into specialized breeds. Dogs with the qualities people valued were treated better than dogs without them, giving them a better chance to survive and pass their desirable characteristics to their offspring. People also saw the importance of having dogs who looked different from their wild counterparts—being able to tell which animals were potential threats and which were pets had obvious advantages. Dogs began to have fewer physical and behavioral traits in common with the wolf.

By 4000 B.C., the ancient Chinese had already developed well-defined types of domestic dogs. The remains of both large and small dogs have been discovered in excavations throughout China. Sacrificial dogs wearing bells have been found buried with people in Chinese tombs circa 1384 B.C. In neighboring Thailand, remains of domesticated dogs have been found dating to about 3500 B.C. These showed signs of tooth marks and charring, suggesting that the dogs had been eaten. Dogs also were used as a food source in southwestern Iran about 6000 B.C. The dogs were about the size of an Irish setter and probably descended from that region's small wolf.

The ancient Egyptians and Babylonians developed many distinct varieties of dogs. A painting, circa 1900 B.C., found in a tomb at Beni Hasan, Egypt, shows a running hound or early version of the greyhound, which was bred for hunting and used throughout Europe and Asia. Other dogs in the painting look like today's Pharaoh hound and one even looks remarkably like a Dachshund with erect ears.

Dogs also were kept by aboriginal tribes throughout the Americas. In the northern parts, these resembled wolves, while in the south, the dogs were more coyote-like. In what is now the southwestern United States, both the Basketmaker Indians and the Pueblo Indians kept small, short-faced dogs and small, long-faced dogs. The Pueblos also had large dogs. In 1921, two mummies of 2,000 year old Basketmaker Indian dogs were found in northwest Arizona. One dog was long-haired and buff-colored, and about the size of a small Collie. It also had the long muzzle of a Collie, with erect ears and a bushy tail. The other dog was Terrier-sized, a short-hair with a shaggy coat, erect ears, a long, bushy tail, and a short muzzle.

Working Dogs and Pets

Throughout ancient times, dogs worked for their masters, performing a variety of tasks. They herded sheep, retrieved game, baited wild animals, pulled carts, and turned cooking spits. While the working dogs of those times were certainly appreciated by their owners, few outside the ruling classes had the resources to afford the luxury of keeping animals merely for pleasure.

Records of dogs as pets in Britain begin in the Middle Ages, about 800 years ago. At that time, pet dogs were pretty much the exclusive domain of the upper classes, and upper class women in particular. Not until the reign of King Charles II, who, along with his brother, James II, was well known for his love of dogs, did it become acceptable for men to appreciate dogs as pets.

Pet dogs continued to be the exclusive domain of the ruling class for the next two hundred years. Dogs were owned by courtiers and some religious authorities. Episcopal monks and nuns also kept pets, much to the chagrin of church authorities, who tried their best to put a stop to the practice.

The first real dog book, published in 1570 as *De Canibus Britannicus* and in 1576 as "of Englishe Dogges," listed seventeen Tudor dog types: "Terrar, Harier, Bloudhound, Gasehunde, Leuiner, Tumbler, Stealer, Setter, Water Spaniel or Fynder, Land Spaniel, Spaniel-gentle or Comforter, Shepards Dog, Mastive or Bande-Dog, Wappe, Turnspit, Dancer." Classified by function, dogs were lumped into three greater categories: hunting dogs, pet dogs (the

Spaniel-gentle was the only pet dog listed) and dogs who did menial work.

The Beginning of the Purebred Dog

The mid 1700s marked the beginning of the first true efforts to develop breeds. In the later years of that century the first pedigrees were maintained. These records were kept for foxhounds, one of the first breeds to be developed for a distinct purpose. The next breed to gain serious attention was the greyhound. Major Topham began publishing a register of matings and births of his greyhounds, thus officially establishing records for the breed.

But the number of breeds known in England continued to be limited. In 1800, only fifteen types of dogs were listed, and the list was still based on the work the dogs did.

By mid-century, forty to sixty breeds were listed in various books, and pet shows were becoming big business in England. The first official dog show was at Newcastle, on June 28, 1859. The Kennel Club was established in 1873 to help combat fraud in the rapidly growing dog show arena. Pedigrees were recorded in the national stud book, first published in 1874. Standards of excellence against which to judge the various breeds were established, and purebred dogs were no longer the exclusive domain of the rich and titled.

The Industrial Revolution altered the way people lived and how they related to dogs. People moved from the country to the city and their work patterns changed. Increasing amounts of leisure time and discretionary income enabled more people to enjoy the "luxury" of keeping pets. Most dog owners and fanciers were urban business people and professionals. Owning a dog was one way the emerging middle class could enjoy some of the privileges of the upper classes that didn't require great wealth or extensive land holdings.

Various breeds went in and out of favor depending upon the whims of royalty. The social climbers latched onto Queen Victoria's favorite breed, the Collie, resulting in major growth of the breed. Another favorite of the Queen, the Pomeranian, enjoyed similar status. The Pug, out of favor for most of the 1800s, had a resurgence in popularity when aristocrats began to breed them—and the black Pug was introduced in 1886.

As purebreds grew in popularity, the ancient working breeds and mixed breeds were in less demand. The dog show circuit encouraged this, as shows were intended to display the best examples of the breeds.

The purebred craze, along with the general notions that dogs could be desirable pets, made a transatlantic voyage during the 1880s and 1890s—Americans joined the movement and exotic breeds began to appear in the United States. The American Kennel Club, patterned after its British counterpart, was formed in 1884.

After 1900, when Gregor Mendel's laws of genetics were accepted, dog breeders began to take a more scientific approach to refining bloodlines. The so-called "true" breeds were established using genetics to improve dogs in specific ways.

The Modern Working Dog

In many parts of the world, dogs continue to work for and with their human masters as they have throughout history. Scientific breeding methods gave rise to such specialized working dogs as the Border Collie, which keeps straying sheep from getting separated from the rest of the flock by staring at them. Under the Border Collie's glare, the perplexed sheep turns around and re-joins its group.

Even in more technologically advanced societies, dogs still perform important tasks. Besides serving as relatively "low-tech" security systems for us and all of our modern conveniences, dogs provide important services to the handicapped, the elderly, and to hospitalized children. Seeing eye dogs are probably the working dogs most familiar to city dwellers. But there are also a growing number of "therapy" dogs working to improve the quality of life for people in situations where they can't own pets themselves.

The Wolf in Your Livingroom

Even after centuries of specialization, dogs are still part of the same genus as wolves. This means that while a wolf and a Pekingese look very different, they—like all dogs—share many common features. For example, the internal structure and form of the wolf and the Pekingese are virtually identical, although the proportions are not. The two share similar teeth, brain shapes, and intestinal tracts. They are hosts to the same parasites, including fleas, ticks, and worms. The young take the same amount of time to develop before birth. The adult Pekingese even resembles a fetal wolf: short face, proportionately large brain case, short legs, big eyes, soft fur. The wolf loses these features before birth or during adolescent growth, but it is consistent with the domestication process for the Pekingese to retain these youthful features.

Social behaviors are also similar in domesticated animals. Dogs act remarkably like wolves in many ways, preferring a den (such as a dog crate) to wide open spaces, socializing with people and other dogs, and respecting the pack leader.

Barking is another behavior common to young wolves that is retained by adult dogs. In the beginning, barking in adult dogs may have been encouraged by humans for the protection it afforded against intruders, or as a tool of communication between man and dog. Whatever the reason, there is no question that barking was perpetuated during the domestication process as adult wolves in the wild rarely bark. It is interesting to note that wolves in captivity can learn to bark, and make many of the same kinds of whining and moaning sounds that dogs do.

A Special Challenge

Domesticated animals live and breed separate and apart from those in the wild. Their wild temperament has been bred out over time, including their defensiveness toward the unfamiliar. To be domesticated, an animal must be somewhat placid and submissive, but not overfearful. We have spent the last 12,000 years working on this, with remarkable results. Unfortunately, there are still rare occasions when the dog's wild side can come out, sometimes with disastrous results. Usually, this is the result of mishandling by people.

Man stops the social development of domesticated animals at an early age. The retention of juvenile characteristics into adulthood, referred to as neoteny, results in dogs retaining a submissiveness similar to that which young wolves give to those with greater status—like their human masters.

We preserve juvenile characteristics in dogs so that they can't fend for themselves, and they are thus forced to depend on us for everything from food to leadership. This is part of the reason that responsible dog ownership is so important—we have altered the species to make them dependent upon us. Adult dogs retain many of the endearing qualities of puppies, which is why they are so loveable. It's also why we have an obligation to provide for them.

The recent spread of wolf/dog interbreeding threatens to undo centuries of domestication efforts in one generation. The domestic canine still has enough connection to its wild antecedent for interbreeding with wild dogs to bring back exactly those characteristics that were bred out because they were incompatible with our human society. Some people mistakenly believe that interbreeding dogs with wolves is a form of conservation, that it will allow wolves facing extinction to survive, although in a somewhat different form. While well intentioned, such people are all too often surprised to find that their pet is much more wolf than dog.

Perpetuating Dogs...
And Preserving Their Wild Cousins

At present, there are over 400 breeds of dogs acknowledged worldwide. Dogs from all over the world are bred and raised in America, where about 52 million dogs are now kept as household pets. But while the domesticated dog continues to thrive, the same cannot be said for its wild cousins.

Like many other wild creatures, wolves, coyotes, jackals, and other wild dogs are threatened by shrinking habitats. While this country was being settled, humans and wild dogs were in direct competition for natural resources. Later, wolves and coyotes were shot, trapped and poisoned when they hunted the sheep and cattle which roamed their old hunting grounds.

This familiar tale has been played out around the world, with the result that only a few thousand grey wolves survive in the wild, and even fewer red wolves. African wild dogs, Asian Dholes and most species of wolf also face extinction unless large wilderness areas in which they can hunt their natural prey are preserved.

Many of these species can still be saved, but it won't be easy. The misconceptions that many people—even dog-lovers—have about wild dogs must be overcome. The evil wolves of fairy tales probably gave rise to many of the myths about wolves. However, there is no recorded instance of a wolf ever killing a human being and wild dogs are no longer the serious threat to livestock that they once were.

Wild dogs make a unique contribution to the beauty and wonderful variety of the natural world. As the stewards of the earth, humanity has an obligation to provide for the survival of its wildlife. And, as owners of their descendants, responsible dog owners owe a special debt to the wolf. It is our hope that dog owners everywhere who love their pets will also learn to respect, appreciate and preserve the special gifts of nature embodied in the wild dog.

Appendix A:
Responsible Dog Owners Association®

~

As a result of the ever changing society in which we live and the more densely populated environment, we experience more poorly behaved, ill-mannered pets. This is a problem for everyone. An uncontrolled dog is a nuisance and a danger to its owners and the neighborhood. Irresponsible dog owners have caused considerable damage and antidog sentiment in the United States. Bad press, mass hysteria and public ignorance about dogs are growing. Heightened national concern over dog problems has prompted municipalities across the nation to propose and enact laws banning or restricting the ownership of dogs.

This prompted a grass roots committee concerned about educating the public on responsible dog ownership to organize in 1987 into a national organization called the Responsible Dog Owners Association® (RDOA). RDOA's major thrust is to educate and promote responsible dog ownership through quality educational programs.

Their first major project was an educational program launched in 1991 through AKC obedience clubs and humane societies across the U.S. The program was designed to help these clubs educate their communities about responsible dog ownership. It allows them to teach everything from how to pick the right puppy to caring for the dog as it grows, including household obedience skills and being a good pet neighbor.

RDOA is engaged in a mass media educational campaign which is designed to reach the 38 percent of the households in the United States that own dogs and prospective dog owners as well. The programs focus on good dog manners, and more importantly, how to be a responsible pet owner. Each aspect of the program conveys what is expected of dog owners as well as "what is" and "is not" acceptable behavior of all dogs in the community. Only when the message is received by millions of pet owners will the problems be resolved.

The overall goal of the organization is to help dog owners become more responsible and reduce the number of unwanted "problem" dogs destroyed in pounds and shelters. This will also reduce the number of negative dog/human-related incidents, such as cases of abuse or improper care, dogs biting people, and dogs running at large causing havoc in the neighborhoods.

The organization also acts as an information resource and can provide guidance to local and state groups which are interested in starting an educational campaign for their communities or governmental bodies.

For those who truly love their dogs and want to help educate their communities about responsible dog ownership, but don't know how, the RDOA can be a starting point.

For more information, contact the RDOA at P.O. Box 173, Fountainville, PA 18923 (215) 249-1377.

Appendix B:
Dogs! with Joan Embery
Computer Software for Responsible Dog Care
Andrew J. Peterson, Ph.D.

~

How can one follow a sufficient discipline of dog care and training in a full life in a busy world?

One excellent way to fulfill all the guidelines for responsible pet care is with a new tool developed with Joan Embery. Joan and a team of professionals at Digital Vistas in San Diego, California, have designed and published a new computer software program which contains all the information and activities necessary to begin and maintain a pattern of responsible care for your dog. It is entitled, *Dogs! with Joan Embery*.

This "smart computer workbook" takes advantage of the computer's ability to quickly calculate scientific recommendations, conveniently store and access vast amounts of reference material, and update your pet's records.

Dogs! with Joan Embery keeps important records, has a library of information, presents scientific data, personalizes a nutrition program, helps with emergencies, and contains enjoyable and educational games.

Dogs! with Joan Embery contains something for everyone in the family. Whether a parent checking expenses and vital care records or a child playing the memory game with the names of various breeds, persons at all developmental levels can benefit from the program. It is never too early to begin training a responsible dog owner.

Dogs! with Joan Embery also contains a wealth of scientific information, including sections on anatomy, selecting a dog, breeds, first-aid, grooming and care.

For information on *Dogs! with Joan Embery* for either IBM-compatible or Macintosh computers, write to Digital Vistas, P.O. Box 2224, Del Mar, CA 92014-1524 or call 1-800-323-PETS.

Index

Joan Embery

Joan Embery was born just a few blocks from the San Diego Zoo. Perhaps coincidentally, animals have always been close to her heart. Joan's parents raised Springer Spaniels and there were always one or two hunting dogs around the house. As a youngster, she often accompanied her uncle, a veterinarian, on his rounds. Joan was allowed to observe him at work in his treatment room. These experiences played a pivotal role in her decision to work with animals when she grew up.

During her first year at San Diego State University, where she studied zoology and telecommunications, she got a job at the San Diego Zoo. At that time, her plan was to use the job to gain practical experience in the field. Nearly twenty-five years later, after numerous television appearances (including the many visits to "The Tonight Show" that made her name a household word), radio interviews, speaking engagements, and wildlife habitat tours, Embery is internationally recognized as the San Diego Zoo's goodwill ambassador and spokesperson for the animals.

She has hosted two television series, "Animal Express" and "Animals of Africa," and has written three other books, *My Wild World* and *Amazing Animal Facts* published by Delacorte and *On Horses* published by William Morrow. In conjunction with the publication of this book, Embery and her husband, Duane Pillsbury, are releasing an innovative computer software program on dogs (see Appendix B).

Embery's experience with dogs includes a wide variety of domestic and exotic canines, from Great Danes to wolves and African hunting dogs. She includes among her closest animal relationships a bond with a female timber wolf that she raised from a pup. She also saved and nursed to health Drifter, a sick stray black Labrador Retriever that arrived on her doorstep nine years ago and only recently passed away. She now has a Yellow Labrador Retriever named Traveler, pictured on the cover of this book.

A nationally recognized lecturer and educator, Joan has traveled the country lecturing on animals. She was also an instructor with the San Diego Dog Obedience Club. In addition, Joan has spoken before such respected groups as the North American Veterinary Conference, numerous humane societies and veterinary colleges.

As someone who has devoted her life to animals and their well-being, Joan cares passionately about the issue of responsible dog ownership. She has been quoted as saying, "When you acquire a pet, you are taking that animal for the rest of its life. You are financially responsible, you are legally responsible and even morally responsible. Morally because you have taken over the pet's life and are in direct control."

An avid horsewoman and winner of many trophies and blue ribbons, Embery and her husband live on a fifty-acre ranch in Lakeside, California. There she raises and trains Quarter Horses, Lipizzaners, Clydesdales and Miniature horses. Joan also has a California State Grand Champion Brahman Bull named Bruiser. She and Duane also share their lives with many other exotic animals, including a cheetah and a zebra from the San Diego Zoo.

Joan would like to thank Audrey and Fon Johnson, highly respected dog trainers and responsible dog care advocates, who provided valuable advice in reviewing this book.

Nan Weitzman

Nan Weitzman is an award-winning writer who holds the distinction of having taught a Bouvier des Flandres to play football and obedience-trained her horse.

She traces her long-standing love of dogs to the happy times she spent helping her grandfather care for his champion field trial dogs. He raised and trained Brittany Spaniels, German Shorthaired Pointers, English Setters, English Pointers, and a rare European pointing breed, the Barque D'Auvergne. Weitzman competes her Irish Wolfhounds and American Staffordshire Terriers in obedience trials and conformation dog shows. All four of her pets are also registered therapy dogs. An accomplished horsewoman, she has been breeding horses for over seventeen years. She owns Quarter Horses and American Paint Horses, which she exhibits in reining competitions.

Weitzman is the president of the Responsible Dog Owners Association (RDOA), a national organization dedicated to promoting responsible pet ownership and fighting discriminatory dog laws. She founded the organization in 1987. Her goal is to educate every dog owner to be a responsible caretaker. As she frequently says, "A poorly behaved, ill-mannered pet is everyone's problem. Only education of owners can solve that problem." She helps educate the public through radio and TV appearances, and with a regular column in *Good Dog!* magazine. She has also created the Responsible Dog Owner's Guide (RDOG), a complete course for community education. It is now being taught throughout the U.S.

Weitzman earned her undergraduate degree in Animal Science at Washington State University. She has a graduate degree in Education (Instructional Training Design) from Penn State University and is working on her doctoral degree in Equine Immunology. She has also worked as a research scientist in which she helped develop immunodiagnostic test kits and monoclonal antibodies.

She would like to thank her parents, Joan and Milton Dauber, who put up with her shenanigans; and Ross Becker, who said, "Stop talking and start writing"; Karen Haas and her red pen; and her husband, Jonathan, who does not mind mud in the house when it rains.